LID

Low Impact Development

a design manual for urban areas

University of Arkansas Community Design Center

FAY JONES SCHOOL OF ARCHITECTURE
UNIVERSITY OF ARKANSAS PRESS
A COLLABORATION
FAYETTEVILLE 2010

Contents

> "
> *...in many cases the first flush of stormwater in an urban area may have a level of contamination much higher than normally present in sewage...*
> "
>
> Craig Campbell and Michael Ogden,
> *Constructed Wetlands in the Sustainable Landscape*

impervious surfaces

What if urban stormwater infrastructure enhanced ecological functioning to serve as a civic asset rather than an environmental liability?

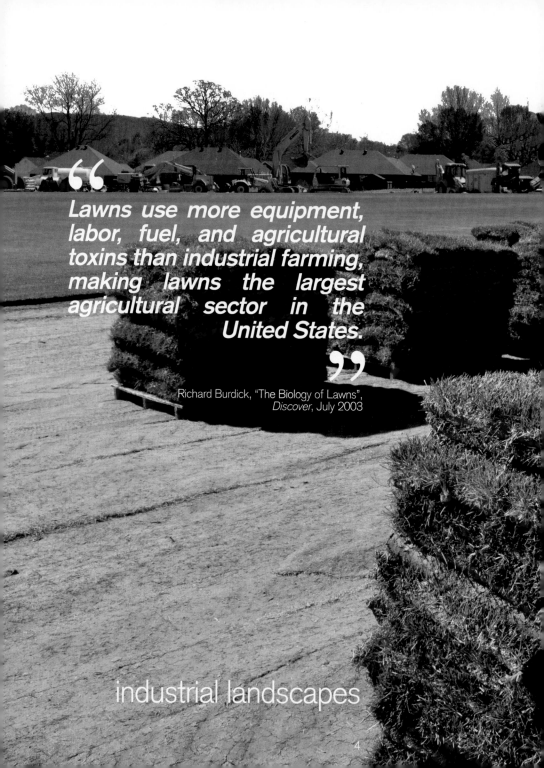

> *Lawns use more equipment, labor, fuel, and agricultural toxins than industrial farming, making lawns the largest agricultural sector in the United States.*
>
> Richard Burdick, "The Biology of Lawns", *Discover*, July 2003

industrial landscapes

> " **By replacing the stream that was once here, the bare and sterile concrete replaces the fecundity of soil and plants. The concrete has just one purpose, ignoring the multiplicity of other purposes served by the landscape it replaced...** "
>
> John Tillman Lyle, "Landscape: Source of Life or Liability", *Reshaping the Built Environment*

urban stream syndrome

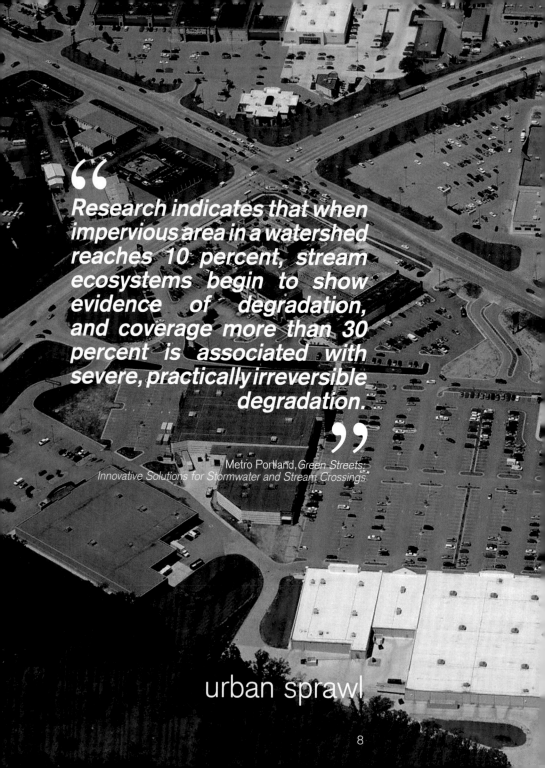

" Research indicates that when impervious area in a watershed reaches 10 percent, stream ecosystems begin to show evidence of degradation, and coverage more than 30 percent is associated with severe, practically irreversible degradation. "

Metro Portland, *Green Streets: Innovative Solutions for Stormwater and Stream Crossings*

urban sprawl

"
death by a
thousand cuts
"

flash flooding

water con

tamination   stream scouring

What Low Impact Development (LID) does is make hard engineering...

work more like soft engineering.

offering the 17 ecosystem services

1. atmospheric regulation
2. climate regulation
3. disturbance regulation
4. water regulation
5. water supply
6. erosion control and sediment retention
7. soil formation
8. nutrient cycling
9. waste treatment
10. pollination
11. species control
12. refugia/habitat
13. food production
14. raw material production
15. genetic resources
16. recreation
17. cultural enrichment

hard engineering

Some believe that ecologically-based stormwater management is unattainable in dense urban areas, but consider the following...

this is a population of 8,000

soft engineering

this is a population of 4,000,000

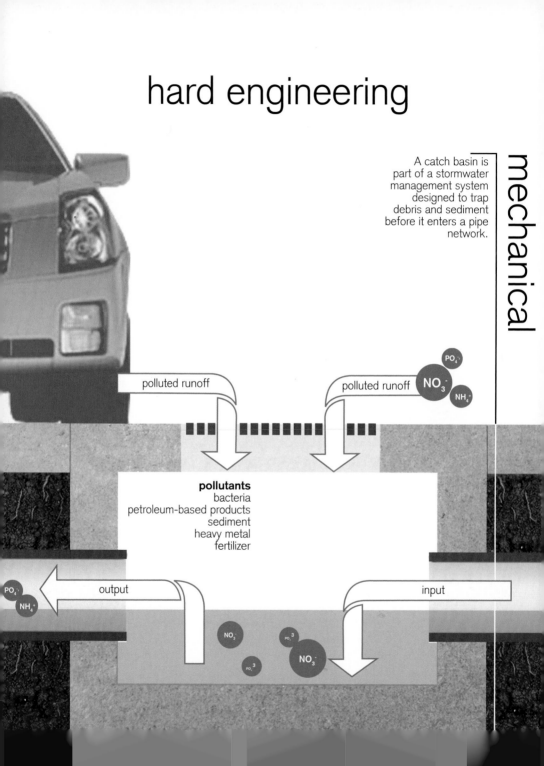

hard engineering

A catch basin is part of a stormwater management system designed to trap debris and sediment before it enters a pipe network.

polluted runoff

polluted runoff

PO_4^-

NO_3^-

NH_4^+

pollutants
bacteria
petroleum-based products
sediment
heavy metal
fertilizer

output

PO_4^-

NH_4^+

input

NO_3^-

PO_4^3

NO_3^-

PO_4^3

soft engineering

biological

Phytoremediation is the mitigation of contaminated soil, water, or air using plants to contain, degrade, or eliminate pollutants.

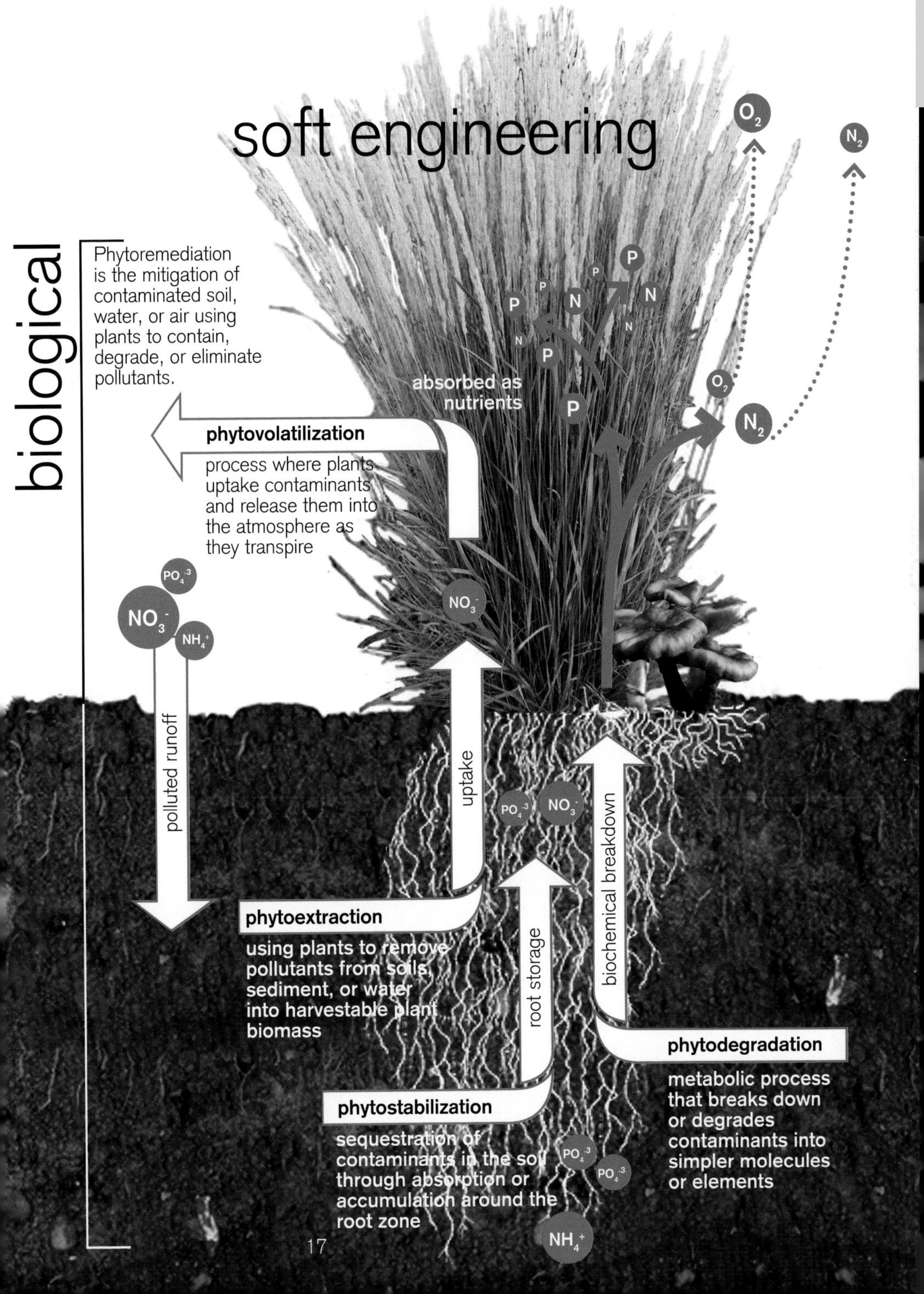

O_2

N_2

P

P

P

N

P

N

P

N

N

absorbed as nutrients

O_2

N_2

N_2

phytovolatilization

process where plants uptake contaminants and release them into the atmosphere as they transpire

PO_4^{-3}

NO_3^-

NH_4^+

NO_3^-

polluted runoff

uptake

PO_4^{-3} NO_3^-

biochemical breakdown

phytoextraction

using plants to remove pollutants from soils, sediment, or water into harvestable plant biomass

root storage

phytostabilization

sequestration of contaminants in the soil through absorption or accumulation around the root zone

PO_4^{-3}

PO_4^{-3}

NH_4^+

phytodegradation

metabolic process that breaks down or degrades contaminants into simpler molecules or elements

17

hard engineering
...just transfers pollution
to another site

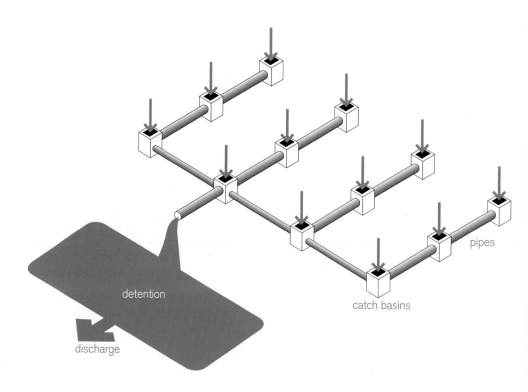

conventional management: "pipe-and-pond" infrastructure
drain, direct, dispatch

soft engineering ...metabolizes pollutants on site—parks, not pipes!

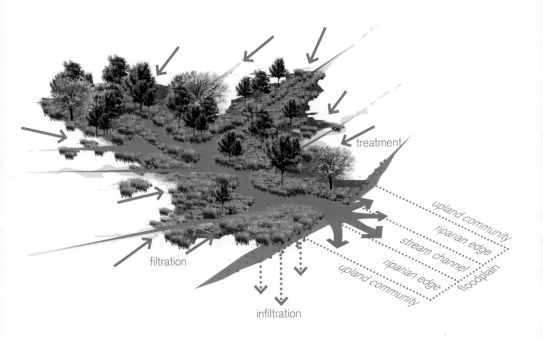

treatment

upland community

riparian edge

stream channel

riparian edge

floodplain

upland community

filtration

infiltration

low impact management: watershed approach
slow, spread, soak

integrating hard engineering

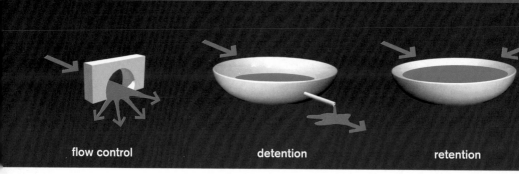

mechanical

flow control   detention   retention

slow ————————————————————→ spr

flow control: The regulation of stormwater runoff flow rates.

detention: The temporary storage of stormwater runoff in underground vaults, ponds, or depressed areas to allow for metered discharge that reduce peak flow rates.

retention: The storage of stormwater runoff on site to allow for sedimentation of suspended solids.

...and soft engineering toward a LID approach

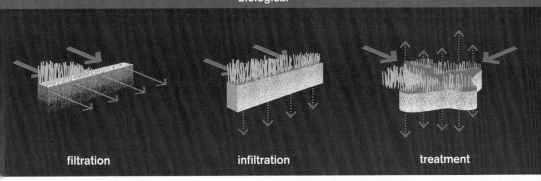

biological

filtration

infiltration

treatment

ead ——————————————————————→ soak

filtration: The sequestration of sediment from stormwater runoff through a porous media such as sand, a fibrous root system, or a man-made filter.

infiltration: The vertical movement of stormwater runoff through soil, recharging groundwater.

treatment: Processes that utilize phytoremediation or bacterial colonies to metabolize contaminants in stormwater runoff.

What is LID?

Low Impact Development (LID) is an ecologically-based stormwater management approach favoring soft engineering to manage rainfall on site through a vegetated treatment network. The goal of LID is to sustain a site's pre-development hydrologic regime by using techniques that infiltrate, filter, store, and evaporate stormwater runoff close to its source. Contrary to conventional "pipe-and-pond" conveyance infrastructure that channels runoff elsewhere through pipes, catchment basins, and curbs and gutters, LID remediates polluted runoff through a network of distributed treatment landscapes.

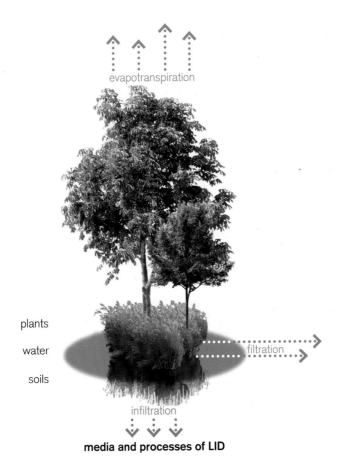

evapotranspiration

plants

water

soils

filtration

infiltration

media and processes of LID

Stormwater infrastructure can be planned to deliver valuable ecological benefits to botanize the city...

Summary:
Botanizing the City

Experts roundly believe that water is the next oil. Both are naturally occurring resources, and ever-increasing demand is creating economic, social, and environmental conflict in allocating their finite supplies. While water problems vary from place to place, access to safe drinking water has become a global challenge. In developing nations, access to potable water is limited—8,000 children worldwide die every day due to illnesses contracted from consuming contaminated water. In arid regions that lack natural water supplies, energy costs from transporting water and resulting scarcities have led to rationing. Large-scale diversions of natural water supplies like those for industrialized farming have depleted continental aquifers, interrupting groundwater recharge, altering stream base-flows, and eroding geological stability. The latter has resulted in subsidence, or the gradual sinking of cities like Mexico City and New Orleans due to water drawdowns. Water ownership and stream management conflicts between neighboring governments have led to water wars and, much like oil, the emergence of water as a market commodity subject to privatization and trade. One of the more pernicious domestic water problems is the effect of rapid urbanization on groundwater quality, particularly in regions with substantial rainfall like the American southeast and northwest. This manual is about the relationship between water and urbanization—specifically stormwater runoff—and the role of "green" development in ensuring good water quality.

While the US does not typically suffer from unclean drinking water, our waterbodies are toxic. The United States Environmental Protection Agency's (USEPA) Index of Watershed Indicators shows that only 16 percent

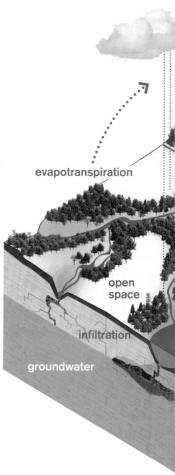

evapotranspiration

open
space

infiltration

groundwater

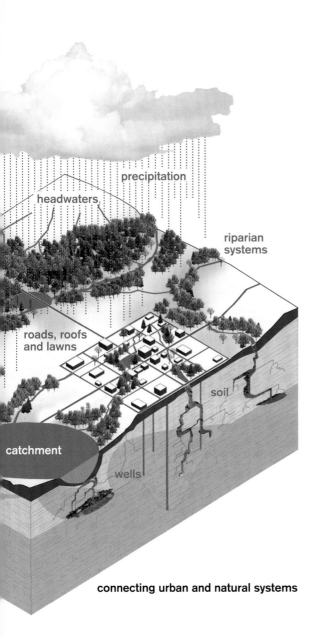

precipitation

headwaters

riparian
systems

roads, roofs
and lawns

soil

catchment

wells

connecting urban and natural systems

of the nation's watersheds exhibit good water quality. Besides discharges from agricultural land uses and site construction, much of this can be attributed to nonpoint source pollution from urban stormwater runoff channeled by impervious surfaces—roofs, sidewalks, parking lots, and roads—during the "first flush" of a storm event.

Indeed the first hour of urban stormwater runoff has a pollution index much higher than that of raw sewage.

Stormwater runoff in our auto-dominated communities is toxic because it concentrates hydrocarbon residues from household and lawn care chemicals, oil, gasoline, brake fluid, asphaltic products in roads and roofs, and heavy metals, which are ultimately deposited into our watersheds. Conventional hard-engineered stormwater management—neither aware nor responsive to runoff's harmful consequences—employs "pipe-and-pond" methods to drain, direct, and dispatch untreated runoff from a site. As with most conventional waste management infrastructure, pipe-and-pond systems simply transfer pollution problems from one place to another.

Besides reduced water quality, stormwater runoff has led to another major pollution problem, widespread stream impairment commonly known as "urban stream syndrome". Urban stream syndrome describes unhealthy stream flow regimes marked by chronic flash flooding, altered stream morphologies, elevated nutrient and contaminant levels, excessive sedimentation, loss of species diversity, and higher water temperatures.

This imbalance in stream metabolism impairs ecological functioning and disrupts the 17 ecological services that a healthy stream delivers (see list p.13). These life-affirming services constitute four basic categories; *provisioning services* that supply food, water, and energy; *regulating services* that purify water, air, and control disease; *supporting services*, which promote nutrient cycling and reproduction; and *cultural services* for intellectual, recreational, and spiritual well being. Escalating costs associated with the loss of these ecological services due

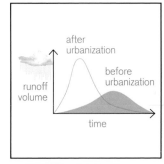

stormwater discharge before and after urbanization

26

to flood damage, property loss from erosion, heat island effect, pollution, and need for irrigation have prompted greater regulatory oversight over nonpoint source pollution and a call for green development solutions. Infrastructure can be designed to provide greater ecological and urban services at lower costs. With LID, streets no longer have to be ecological liabilities, and stream and lake ecological functioning are enhanced.

Water and land should be developed in harmony. New LID practices based on ecological soft-engineering can mitigate the deleterious impacts of urbanization on the environment, particularly in the substitution of natural ground cover or porous media for impervious surfaces.

Shockingly, the rate of increase in impervious surfaces has exceeded the rate of population growth by 500 percent over the last 40 years.

From Individual Facilities to Networks: BMP to LID
Best Management Practice (BMP) has been commonly used in conventional hard-engineering to identify lot-based management facilities such as a detention pond. However, BMPs are focused more on engineering rather than planning. In recognizing the need to comprehensively address stormwater runoff, the USEPA has recently redefined the term as "a practice or combination of practices that are an effective, practicable means of preventing or reducing the amount of pollution generated by nonpoint sources". BMPs now address stormwater runoff quantity and quality by employing both mechanical and biological processes.

From the lot to the neighborhood, city, and region, BMPs, or LID facilities, are connected in a distributed network to reduce and treat urban stormwater runoff before it enters receiving waterbodies. LID facilities are combined with smart growth practices, such as compact, walkable neighborhoods and open space preservation (see www.epa.gov/smartgrowth), resulting in LID. Successful LID requires participation from property owners, developers, cities, and regulatory agencies in a comprehensive planning process. Everyone has an important role to play.

27

The Three Tenets of the Watershed Approach

Enhance Landscape Biodiversity

Between turf and asphalt we have industrialized our ground surfaces, eliminating local plant and soil communities necessary for natural hydrological cycling. LID technologies rely on biogeochemical rather than low-service mechanical processes to manage and treat stormwater runoff. LID promotes the use of xeriscapes, or water conserving landscapes of drought-resistant plants to maximize the delivery of ecological services in development. Turf grasses kill biodiversity because the standard lawn is dependent on a regimen of chemical fertilizers and herbicides to maintain its plant monoculture.

soil as sponge

Maximize Water Infiltration and Eliminate Runoff

Urbanization has caused the loss of wetlands, forest, vegetation cover, and soil humus, all of which constitute a watershed's carrying capacity to slow, spread, and soak stormwater, creating stable hydrological functioning. LID promotes the use of pervious surfaces and networked plant communities to remediate pollution and peak flow of runoff after a storm.

Engineer Hydrology in Distributed Networks

Conventional hard-engineered stormwater infrastructure concentrates runoff in detention facilities then dispatches polluted runoff to another site, simply moving waste problems around. Instead, LID performance is optimized when runoff is treated through a robust network with high connectivity, redundancy, and distribution.

excessive impervious surfacing
Streets, parking lots, and roofs can be designed as gardens to slow, spread, and soak stormwater runoff.

...compare best management practices to urban challenges

robust plant communities

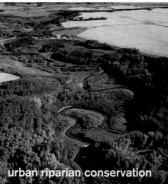

urban riparian conservation

balanced growth

lack of biological functioning
Productive vegetation within cities provides ecological services not attainable with the decorative suburban lawn and impervious surfaces.

urban stream syndrome
If forested parks are the "lungs of the city" as landscape architects have claimed, healthy urban riparian (stream) systems are the "kidneys of the city".

urban sprawl
Urban sprawl infills wetlands and clearcuts sites, which may maximize development efficiencies, but destroys ecological or natural capital. Good urban land-use planning reflects, rather than destroys, ecosystems that structure the biological patterns and processes of a place.

The LID Watershed Approach

The first law of ecology is that everything is connected to everything else. Each plant, animal, and micro-organism has an integrated relationship within its ecosystem. All organisms, as biotic elements, create reciprocal relationships with their abiotic environments. Ecological thinking, then provides a platform for understanding the synergistic processes in LID.

LID employs the "watershed approach", a holistic stormwater management system based on watersheds as planning units, rather than political jurisdictions and legal property boundaries. The approach integrates economics, ecological science, and social dynamics in development processes within the context of a watershed. LID works by utilizing the natural processes of the water cycle governing watersheds. Just as with nature, LID treatment networks are designed not to exceed the *carrying capacity* of the site's landscape. Though LID landscapes share common technologies called "best management practices", LID is ultimately a place-bound approach dependent upon the integration of local soil, plant, and hydrological communities. In the same way we know what town and state we live in, we should also know what watershed we live in, and how personal and collective activities impact natural resources critical to our well being.

transporters

Soils and Plants as Treatment Facilities

LID site design begins with hydrological modeling based upon local geography, soil types, vegetation, and watershed catchment patterns. Conventional hard-engineering, based on universal protocols for runoff evacuation, favors costly peak demand design over context-sensitive design. LID, on the other hand, is a high-performance technology

soils as natural water treatment facilities

pollinators

decomposers

digesters

exchangers and digesters

aerators and tillers

nutrient cycler

based on a site specific design solution tailored to place, but requires more planning. While LID applications were pioneered in land-rich suburban contexts, they are adaptable to urban densities. Such densities may entail hybrid systems, combining conventional and ecological engineering, that meet municipal requirements for managing 100-year storm events.

LID employs ecological engineering to store and treat polluted runoff through biological processes that occur in healthy plant and soil communities. Microbial processes, particularly those conducted throughout the root zones of plant and soil media, break down volatile compounds in pollutants, rendering them inert. As with any organic process, optimal functioning of a LID network is both scale and time-dependent, requiring pulsed and incremental water inputs.

Solving for Impervious Surfaces: Soil as Sponge

Native soils play a critical role in the storage, conveyance, and treatment of stormwater. Pores and fractures comprising soil structure act as conduits that carry water from the surface to groundwater and aquifers below. Soil structure is formed when soil biota and organic matter chemically and physically bind mineral particles into aggregates. Depending on location, six to twelve inches of soil high in organic, biologically active material, known as topsoil lays atop a substrate. Both texture and structure determine pore space available for air and water circulation, erosion resistance, plant root penetration, and ease of tillage. Clay, for instance, offers the least infiltration potential of soil types, while sand offers the most.

Soil moisture, intermittent water, and humus serve as transitional fluids for cycling plant nutrients through the soil profile. Consider how native prairies and forests function in the absence of tillage and commercial fertilizers. They are tilled by soil organisms, like worms, not by machinery.

Applying LID: Soils and Site

LID requires detailed analyses of site soils, particularly at LID facility locations to determine hydric soil types and

hydrologic soil groups

D — High runoff potential with slow rate of infiltration. Characteristics include clay, soils with a high water table, soils with claypan or a clay layer near surface, and shallow soils over impervious surface types.

C — Slow infiltration and rate of water transmission potential. Characteristics include silty loam with a layer resisting water transmission or soils with moderately fine to fine texture types.

B — Moderate infiltration and rate of water transmission potential. Characteristics include well-drained sandy loam and moderately fine texture to course gravel types.

A — Low runoff potential and high infiltration rates that offer a high rate of water transmission. Characteristics include deep, well-drained sand and gravel types.

increasing permeability →

clay

silt

sand

clay

silty clay

clay loam

silty clay loam

loam

silt loam

silt

soil texture triangle

33

infiltration rates. Depending on the soil type and structure, 10 to 40 percent of annual precipitation can be infiltrated to replenish groundwater. Optimum LID planning places new impervious surfaces over less permeable soils, while highly permeable soils desirable for LID should be used for infiltration and treatment. Soil surveys and borings conducted by a certified professional designate soil hydrologic classes (A, B, C, or D) based on compaction, texture, depth, and other characteristics. Although a "loam" is considered to be an ideal soil for permeability, LID design employs the site's soil profile and avoids wholesale soil amendment. Let the site dictate design. However, a small scale project like a rain garden may not need a detailed soil analysis, when the study of soil maps (see websoilsurvey.nrcs.usda.gov) and a percolation test will suffice. A percolation test can be conducted to determine the soil's infiltration rate measured in minutes per inch (for information on how to conduct percolation tests see www.percolationtest.com). LID principles regarding soils are as follows:

before construc

Before Construction

Develop an erosion and sediment control plan. Conduct soil borings at LID facility areas to identify soil type and the depth of groundwater, or water table. Conduct a percolation test to determine the soil's infiltration rate. Develop a "no compaction zone" plan based on location of LID facilities and high compaction probability areas (typically soil with high percolation rates) to prevent heavy site equipment use in these areas.

During Construction

Employ erosion and sediment control devices. Avoid compaction by implementing the "no compaction zone" plan. Avoid site work during rainfall—wet soils are more vulnerable to compaction.

After Construction

Implement a soil enhancement regimen through the use of soil amendments. To generate microbial communities add compost, and for infiltration add sand. Manage LID facility areas by removing litter annually to prevent clogging (see "Management, Not Maintenance" pp. 206-211).

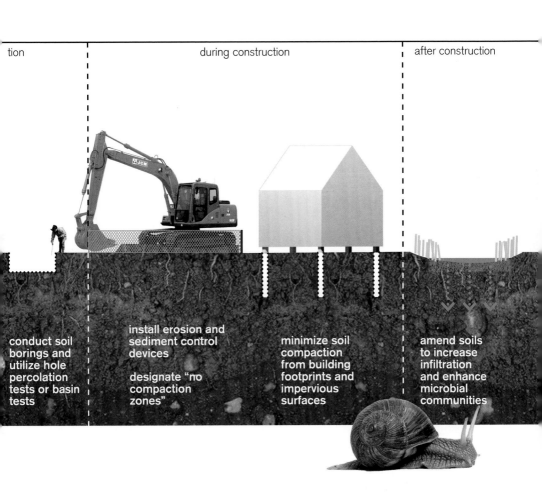

tion | during construction | after construction

conduct soil borings and utilize hole percolation tests or basin tests

install erosion and sediment control devices

designate "no compaction zones"

minimize soil compaction from building footprints and impervious surfaces

amend soils to increase infiltration and enhance microbial communities

Solving for Biological Functioning: Plants as Filters

The root systems of plants naturally filter and treat stormwater, while the matrix of roots, stems and leaves attenuate and encourage infiltration. Plant leaves and branches also intercept rainfall, managing the amount of water that reaches the ground. Roots break up rock and soil, indirectly aiding in infiltration and encouraging soil tilling. These actions facilitate soil development and microbial colonization.

Plants link soils to the atmosphere. Plant species interact with fungi, bacteria, insects and other living things in soil to form unique communities. Plant communities adapt to conditions that define their metabolisms. For instance, wetland communities differ from deciduous forests based upon extremes in soil moisture, temperature regimes, rainfall, and day length. These plant communities are the foundation of ecosystem services. Understanding the interactions between plants and their soil communities provides a basis for designing ecosystem services.

The transitional areas between plant communities, called ecotones, are the most productive and biodiverse areas on Earth. One example are riparian buffers—facultative plant communities at the stream's edge connecting land and water—that facilitate diverse ecosystem services. Just like riparian buffers, LID facilities require facultative plants with the capacity to tolerate wet and dry cycles. Facultative vegetation is also highly productive, capable of controlling sediment deposition and regulating shallow water temperature necessary for important land-water enzymatic exchange and aquatic wildlife habitat.

Applying LID: Plants and Site

When the hydrology of a site is characterized, the plant community should be inventoried and compared to the ecoregion. The conservation and enhancement of existing native facultative vegetation and wetland plant communities for stormwater management is a central principle of LID design. Native plants increase biodiversity crucial for ecosystem resiliency, encourage phytoremediation, and promote healthy microbial communities. Non-native,

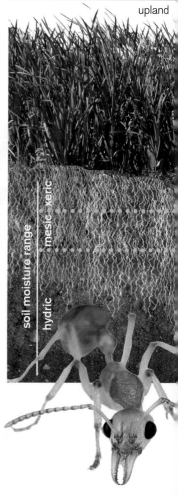

upland

soil moisture range

xeric

mesic

hydric

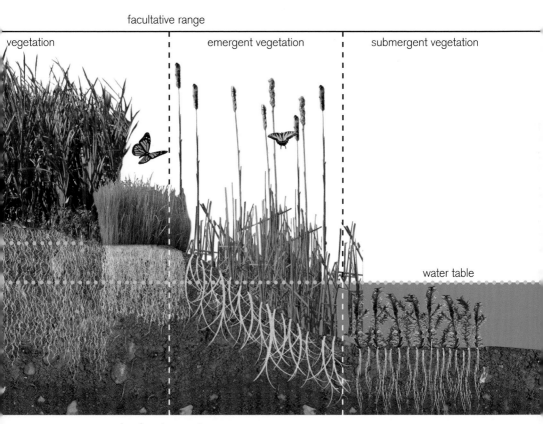

facultative range

vegetation | emergent vegetation | submergent vegetation

water table

land-water ecotone

non-invasive plants can be used, but native plants are better at establishing synergies with local biotic communities.

Natural adaptation to local conditions is an important process in ecosystem development. Ecosystems mature through a process of plant succession, where establishment or pioneering plant communities like native grasses and small woody shrubs evolve into more complex softwood and hardwood forests when left unattended. Each stage in the maturation process delivers ever-increasing ecological services with less energy use (e.g., redwood forests have one of the lowest energy demands per unit of biomass). LID principles regarding vegetation are as follows:

Protect Pre-Development Vegetation
Protect and preserve existing native vegetation and urban forests during construction, particularly along waterbody edges. Heavy equipment should not be allowed to park on or travel across critical root zones.

Prevent Erosion During and After Construction
Do not clearcut a site. Install erosion control blankets, lay straw or seed native grasses like buffalograss and wild rye to temporarily stabilize stockpiled topsoil (see native grasses www.fhwa.dot.gov/environment/rdsduse/ar.htm).

Restore Ecological Services
Re-establish critical ecological habitat and wetlands as appropriate for regional and local conditions.

Solving for Urban Stream Syndrome: Water as Solvent

Nutrient overloading from nitrogen, phosphorous, and potassium used in industrialized landscaping practices (lawn fertilizers, insecticides, and herbicides), as well as animal wastes, and leaks from sanitary sewers impair natural hydrological cycling. Nutrient concentrations transported in stormwater runoff can result in heavy algae growth, which lowers dissolved oxygen levels leading

year 1: initial planting and soil amendment if necessary, root systems begin to establish

establishment stage

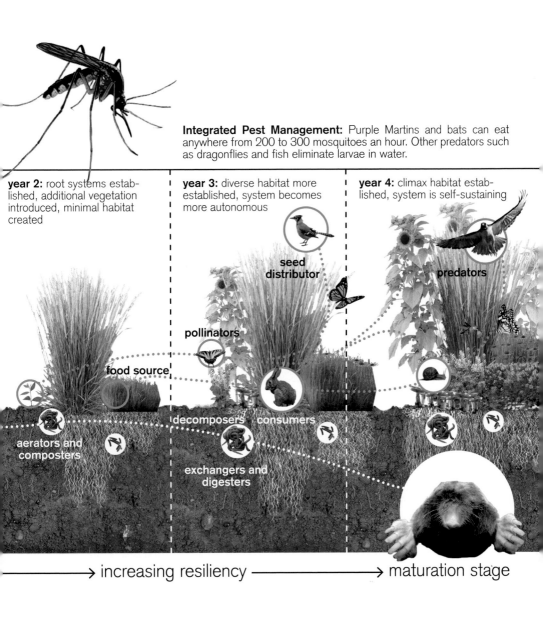

Integrated Pest Management: Purple Martins and bats can eat anywhere from 200 to 300 mosquitoes an hour. Other predators such as dragonflies and fish eliminate larvae in water.

year 2: root systems established, additional vegetation introduced, minimal habitat created

year 3: diverse habitat more established, system becomes more autonomous

year 4: climax habitat established, system is self-sustaining

seed distributor

predators

pollinators

food source

decomposers   consumers

aerators and composters

exchangers and digesters

→ increasing resiliency ———————→ maturation stage

to eutrophication most common in lakes. Bacteria from organic matter, such as garbage, and pet and yard wastes, decomposes in surface waters, reducing water quality. Oil, toxic substances, and heavy metals from automobiles, pesticides, and building materials are harmful to biological systems and aquatic life. LID networks render these toxins inert.

Applying LID: Water and Site

Designing for LID requires an understanding of hydrology, the science of water occurrence, distribution and movement on a given area. The initial phase of LID design must characterize the site's natural hydrology, connectivity up and down stream, location within the catchment area, and on-site flow paths.

Understanding the amount of precipitation that typically occurs in an area is important for site planning and stormwater design. Precipitation occurs in different durations, amounts, and intensities, classified as storm events. A storm event is referred to in terms of a year, such as 10-year storm event. This terminology can be misleading, as a 10-year event does not indicate that it will occur once every 10 years, but rather that there is a 1 in 10, or 10 percent chance of that storm occurring in any given year. In other words, while there is only a one percent chance of a 100-year storm event happening every year, it does not mean that a 100-year storm event can't happen twice in the same year.

LID Design: Redundancy, Resiliency, Distribution

Ill-planned urban development results in the loss and fragmentation of ecological habitats, as well as the related loss of ecological biodiversity. A set of specific design principles can increase the level of ecological services in urban infrastructure. These principles of redundancy, diversity, and distribution model the ecological dynamics necessary to optimize the landscape's carrying capacity and resiliency. Application of these design principles are the foundation for design of a LID treatment network that can effectively slow, spread, and soak runoff.

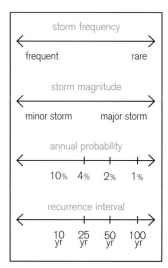

understanding storm event classifications

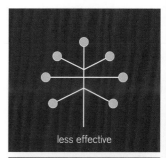

less effective

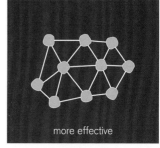

more effective

redundancy

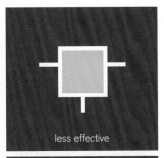

less effective

more effective

resiliency

less effective

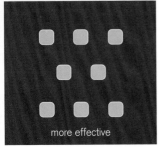

more effective

distribution

Redundancy

To avoid systemic failure (i.e., flooding) facility redundancy is important in LID design. While some facilities may work well in isolation for first flush and small storm events, a distributed circuit of facilities creates redundancy by connecting facilities in multiple routes. The alternate routes in a network reduce the effects of gaps, increasing performance and general levels of service. Hybrid conventional and ecological engineering systems may be connected through surface facilities and underground conveyance to address sites with poor soils and for larger storm events up to a 100-year event.

Resiliency

To maximize ecological benefits, LID design should incorporate multiple LID facilities (see "What are the LID Facilities" pp. 142-187) with different levels of service. Using an array of LID facilities that slow, spread, and soak stormwater assures full treatment capacity and resiliency in the system. Facilities that simply control flow and store stormwater should accompany more robust facilities that filter, infiltrate, and treat stormwater.

To optimize resiliency, healthy ecosystems are readily adaptable to metabolic alterations brought on by external or internal disturbances. Biological diversity increases resiliency, enabling LID networks to withstand shocks or perturbations, rebuilding themselves when necessary. Design for optimum resiliency maximizes interfaces like those in natural systems avoiding the system rigidity of conventional engineering.

Distribution

Distribution, or a dispersed spatial arrangement of LID facilities, optimizes the full carrying capacity of a site and avoids pitfalls associated with concentration. Water quality and quantity functioning are cumulative so that even very small facilities provide compounding benefits to the overall network. Usually, several small facilities will provide greater treatment and more diverse habitat than one large facility, while accommodating sensitive areas.

LID: From Facility to Network

The conventional development process separates design, administration, and financing of the horizontal infrastructure from individual property development. When speaking of ecological practices, Wendell Berry reminds us in *The Gift of Good Land*, that "a good solution in one pattern preserves the integrity of the pattern that contains it". Recalling Berry's adage, the LID watershed approach entails holistic planning through the nestling of scales among the building, property, street, and open space.

Each development component offers intrinsic and scalable stormwater cycling and conservation technologies. Component interfaces—or "development ecotones"— are particularly opportunistic areas for creating an urban LID network. Yet, fragmentation in the development and regulatory processes present major obstacles to such integrated planning. A major obstacle includes the lack of integrated asset management, where regulatory agencies for roads, stormwater management, utilities, and landscape each work in isolation, often with contradictory mandates. Other obstacles include difficulty in funding first costs and additional maintenance costs regardless of favorable lifecycle cost assessments that will result in multiple returns on investment. Nonetheless, each component suggests within its realm a unique agency among property owners, developers, cities, and regions with potential for game-changing impacts. LID requires individuals to implement projects, but it takes a region to make it work.

lots: LID lots infiltrate stormwater through reduction or elimination of impervious surfaces and replacement of turf grass with productive landscapes.

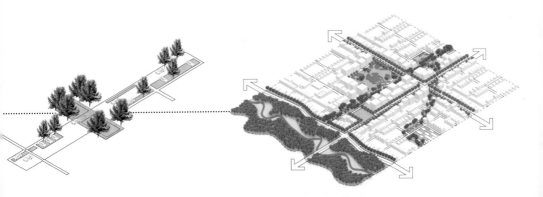

streets: LID streets are green streets reducing and filtering runoff as it enters public space while enhancing the quality of place.

networks: LID networks contain treatment facilities connected to regionally scaled systems of stormwater management.

How can we implement LID?

LID concepts are scalable to various sized projects and land-use types. Dividing urban development into its constituent components—building, property, street and open space—illustrates stakeholder action opportunities within each component. The goal is not just to minimize impact, but to develop regenerative and productive urban landscapes that continually renew ecosystem functioning.

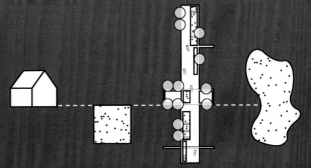

building
pp. 46-57

design the
building as a
net energy
producer that
recharges
groundwater
and harvests
rainwater

property
pp. 58-89

substitute
an ecologi-
cally-based
stormwater
treatment
system for
an otherwise
decorative
landscape

street
pp. 90-123

design the
street as a
garden to
achieve traffic
calming and
stormwater
management

open space
pp. 124-141

comprehen-
sively plan
open space
as a green
network
that delivers
vital ecologi-
cal services at
the scale of a
watershed

bu

conventional
drain, direct, dispatch

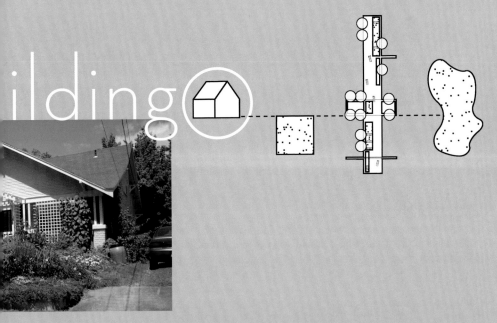

ilding ⌂ ○

low impact
slow, spread, soak

LID Overview

building

Buildings present ready opportunities for harvesting stormwater runoff from roofs through small-scale embedded technologies. LID facilities are one aspect of "smart building" development that optimize feedback between environment and building to achieve net energy production, or regenerative development (versus sustainable development, which is carbon neutral). LID facilities are chosen according to the level of ecological service desired. The simplest service is groundwater recharge from roof stormwater runoff. Gutters and leaders that channel rainwater create concentrated discharges and are avoided in favor of devices that slow, spread, and soak rainwater throughout the site. A higher level of service involves vegetated or green roofs, which absorb and evaporate rainwater through a cultivated plant and soil community. Green roofs are superior building insulators, minimizing heating and cooling demands. Green walls minimize solar gain during the summer and wind loading during the winter.

retention

Rainwater harvesting offers three basic levels of service, involving storage cisterns with options for treatment. The simplest service is rainwater reuse for outdoor landscape irrigation. A more complex harvesting service incorporates a greywater building supply with additional treatment for non-potable water uses like toilet flushing and landscape irrigation. The highest level of service involves harvesting for potable (drinking) water which requires UV light disinfection for a private water system, and when combined with water from a public utility includes proper back-flow prevention.

infiltration

Placement of LID facilities on a building site should be carefully considered. Infiltration and treatment facilities can be used next to a building to capture roof runoff. Infiltration facilities, however, should be located at least 10 feet away from buildings, as they may cause the shrinking and swelling of soils, which can negatively affect foundations.

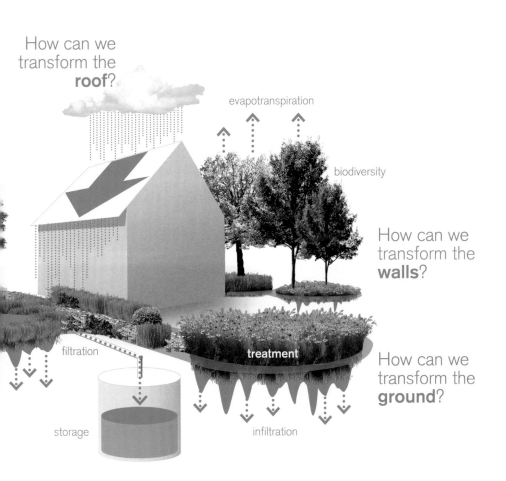

How can we
transform the
roof?

evapotranspiration

biodiversity

How can we
transform the
walls?

filtration

treatment

How can we
transform the
ground?

storage

infiltration

Roof Materials

asphalt/fiberglass shingle

Stormwater runoff from these roofs have high levels of pollution; treatment is needed at the wall and/or ground. If harvesting is desired do not use to irrigate edible landscapes or for potable needs.

- Harvesting Potential: Low
- Heat Island Mitigation: Low
- Initial Cost: Low
- Durability: 15-20 years

membrane roof system

Membrane roofs, like EPDM, modified bitumen, and tar and gravel, are petroleum-based and have high levels of pollutants; treatment is needed at the wall and/or ground. If harvesting is desired do not use to irrigate edible landscapes or for potable needs.

- Harvesting Potential: Low
- Heat Island Mitigation: Low
- Initial Cost: Low-Medium
- Durability: 10-30 years

wood shingle

Leaching from treated wood products may contain toxins and carcinogens. Make every effort to use products made from cedar since it is typically untreated and thus a safe harvesting alternative.

- Harvesting Potential: Moderate
- Heat Island Mitigation: Moderate
- Initial Cost: Medium
- Durability: 10-20 years

alert on harvesting rainwater

When considering rainwater harvesting, keep in mind that petroleum-based roofing and treated wood products leach toxins. Studies have shown that these products are known to cause cancer and mental defects. Harvested rainwater from these surfaces should only be used for ornamental landscape irrigation.

...one inch of rainfall on a 1,000 square-foot roof yields about 623 gallons of water.

clay tile roof
Stormwater runoff from a clay tile roof may produce minor sediment. Clay tiles can offer high albedo surfaces for heat island mitigation. Clay roof tiles have excellent harvesting potential.
- Harvesting Potential: High
- Heat Island Mitigation: Moderate
- Initial Cost: Medium
- Durability: 50-75 years

metal roof
Stormwater runoff from a metal roof has very low pollutant levels. Metal roofs have excellent harvesting potential.
- Harvesting Potential: High
- Heat Island Mitigation: High
- Initial Cost: Medium to High
- Durability: 40-60+ years

vegetated roof
Also known as a "green roof," they can treat and retain 60-100% of the stormwater they receive. Other benefits include improved air quality, heat island mitigation, and urban biodiversity. (see "Vegetated Roof" pp. 170-171)
- Harvesting Potential: High
- Heat Island Mitigation: High
- Initial Cost: High
- Durability: 40+ years

→ safe harvesting potential
Harvesting rainwater from these surfaces is safe for use on edible landscapes because they do not pose contamination risks, but will require filtration and disinfection for potable (drinking) water uses.

Wall Facilities

building

eliminating gutters | rain chain

rainwater harvesting
Connecting a cistern or tank to easiest solution for harvesting must be protected from growth and screened openings larvae propagation. Residential from 100 to 2,500 gallons (see 56-57). Metal or green roofs harvesting. Any overflow should facility. *Rainwater Harvesting*

disconnecting/replacing/eliminating gutters
If you have a gutter system and it's connected with pipes to the street storm drain, disconnect it and keep stormwater on site. If gutters are removed, be sure that the drip edge directs runoff to LID facilities that slow and spread stormwater runoff. Compared to rain leaders, rain chains have better attenuation capacity for **one to two-year storm events**, however, during **10 to 100-year storm events** ground based facilities will be needed to attenuate beyond the capacity of rain chains. This illustrates the importance of redundancy where each facility works in tandem to support the other. No facility is left isolated.

rain barrel

In some cases, harvested rainwater is better or equal to the quality of well or municipal water supplies.

vegetated screen

vegetated wall

an existing gutter system is the stormwater. However, cisterns sunlight to prevent algae are needed to prevent mosquito cisterns typically store anywhere "How to Harvest Rainwater" pp. are best suited for rainwater be diverted to an on-site LID pp. 158-159

rainwater cistern

vegetated screens and walls

Vegetated walls and screens are expensive LID facilities. However, they offer collateral benefits such as higher air quality, reduced heat island effect, building insulation and energy efficiency, aesthetic appeal, and filtration of roof stormwater runoff that can be conveyed or harvested. *Vegetated Wall* pp. 168-169

Ground Facilities
building

splash
block

rock
swale

below-grade storage
Connecting below-grade
gutter system facilitates out of
on-grade rainwater harvesting
be protected from sunlight
and screened openings are
larvae propagation (see "How
56-57). Metal or green roofs
harvesting. Any overflow
site LID facility. *Rainwater*

softscapes
For conventional roofs, splash blocks and rock swales can
transition vertical stormwater flow in tandem with LID facilities
to aid in horizontal network distribution. Rock swales slow and
convey stormwater runoff, acting like a dry creek bed that
receives and distributes concentrated runoff. Where steep
grades are a concern, the rock swale may need to be lined with
geotextile to prevent undercutting. For larger roof areas, wide
rock swales and flow control devices, like level spreaders, will
be needed. *Flow Control Devices* pp.148-149

dry well
filter

storage devices to an existing
sight rainwater harvesting. Like
systems, stormwater must
to prevent algae growth
needed to prevent mosquito
to Harvest Rainwater" pp.
are best suited for rainwater
should be diverted to an on-
Harvesting pp. 158-159

rain
garden   xeriscaping

below-grade
cistern

enhanced urban ecologies

By implementing a biodiverse treatment train across the
property, stormwater can be filtered, infiltrated, and treated
to improve water quality. These facilities can be designed as
habitat for local pollinators and seed distributors, such as bees,
butterflies, and migratory birds. LID landscapes are highly
productive and self-organizing, and provide greater aesthetic
value than turf lawns at a fraction of the required maintenance
(see "What are the LID Facilities" pp. 142-143).

How to Harvest Rainwater

building

Rainwater harvesting consists of up to six primary components, depending on the targeted level of water quality. These components are catchment, conveyance, filtration, storage, distribution, and purification. The amount of water collected depends on catchment size, surface texture, surface porosity, slope conditions of the roof, and annual rainfall. Regardless of the catchment surface material, a transmission loss of 10 to 70 percent should be expected due to runoff material absorption or percolation, evaporation, and inefficiencies in the collection process. The first flush of rainwater after a dry period should be diverted from the catchment system as it will be contaminated with dust, mosses, pesticides, bird droppings, etc. When considering rainwater harvesting there are a couple things to know: 1) check your local codes as rainwater harvesting is illegal in some areas; and 2) know your options, as system applications range from landscape irrigation, greywater uses, like flushing toilets, to potable options that supply buildings with drinking water. *Rainwater Harvesting* pp. 158-159

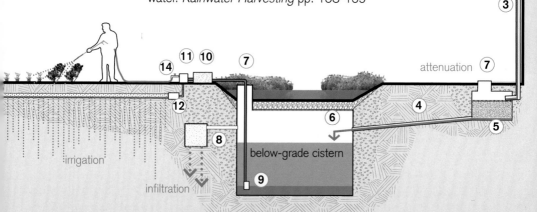

irrigation

attenuation 7

infiltration

below-grade cistern

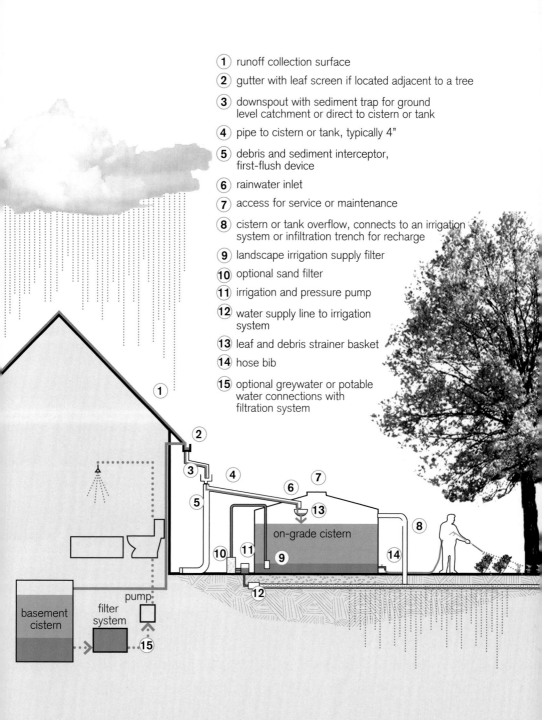

1. runoff collection surface
2. gutter with leaf screen if located adjacent to a tree
3. downspout with sediment trap for ground level catchment or direct to cistern or tank
4. pipe to cistern or tank, typically 4"
5. debris and sediment interceptor, first-flush device
6. rainwater inlet
7. access for service or maintenance
8. cistern or tank overflow, connects to an irrigation system or infiltration trench for recharge
9. landscape irrigation supply filter
10. optional sand filter
11. irrigation and pressure pump
12. water supply line to irrigation system
13. leaf and debris strainer basket
14. hose bib
15. optional greywater or potable water connections with filtration system

on-grade cistern

basement cistern

filter system

pump

pro

lawn

parking

lawn

conventional
drain, direct, dispatch

perty

parking

low impact
slow, spread, soak

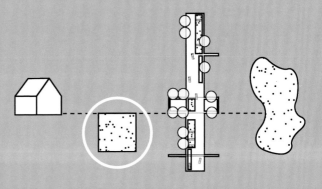

LID Overview

property

In low to moderate urban densities, the property parcel is the fundamental unit for implementation of LID, as stormwater runoff should be filtered and attenuated on-site in lot-based strategies. Since turf and asphalt are the biggest culprits in the elimination of plant and soil communities necessary for natural hydrological cycling, property owners play a pivotal role in realizing successful urban LID projects. LID solutions for both the lawn and the parking lot are addressed in this section, illustrating strategies for minimizing use of impervious surfaces, incorporating LID facilities, and increasing on-site stormwater runoff management.

runoff

How can we introduce **productive landscapes**?

Lawn

In Fritz Haeg's *Edible Estates: Attack on the Front Lawn*, essayist Diana Balmori states that the "smooth manicured lawn demands a monoculture of one or two species of grasses: every other plant must be carefully removed or exterminated." Since the primary goal of the industrial lawn is to achieve an unnatural greenness among non-native grasses, significant quantities of chemical-based resources are required. Adapting lawns to local climate and use of native vegetation not only mitigates stormwater pollution, it also saves municipally treated potable water from being wasted on yard irrigation. Indeed, the lawn can treat and infiltrate stormwater, as well as become a productive landscape to grow food.

How can we increase **on-site infiltration**?

LID is scalable from the lot, to the block, and to the neighborhood. While their plant-based treatment networks function similarly, block and neighborhood scale configurations require cooperative arrangements among owners. LID utility easements across individual properties

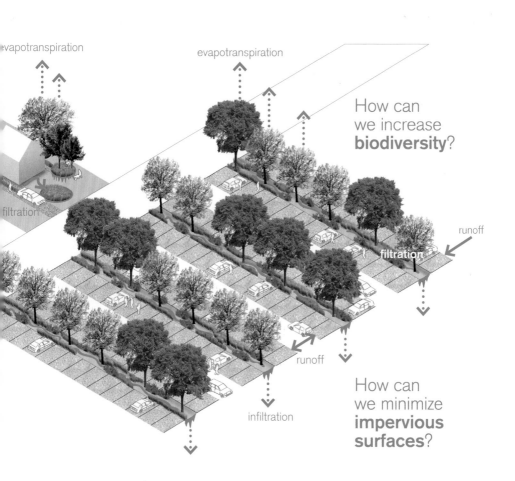

evapotranspiration

evapotranspiration

How can
we increase
biodiversity?

filtration

filtration

runoff

runoff

infiltration

How can
we minimize
**impervious
surfaces**?

can ensure integrated infrastructure functioning, especially in urban areas where small-lot parcels are not large enough to manage stormwater runoff. Shared LID landscapes add a premium to property value, as the acclaimed Village Homes neighborhood in Davis, California has notably shown. Village Homes marks a growing trend in the development of natural resource utilities focused on closed-loop water treatment and cycling.

The Parking Lot

Since most municipal development codes specify 1,500 square feet of automobile parking for every 1,000 square feet of retail space, commercial parking lots are typically oversized. Parking lots can be reconceived as public stormwater treatment gardens with curb appeal, particularly when automobiles are absent.

Tree coverage should be a primary principle for both new and adapted parking lots. Trees provide human scale, reduce stormwater volume, and when planned accordingly, are excellent wayfinding elements. Tree selection should ensure mature canopy coverage of at least 50 percent of paved surfaces to help mitigate the heat island effect. Tree islands should be a minimum size of one parking space, typically 10'x 20', to promote adequate rainwater percolation to the root system (see "Designing for Urban Trees" pp. 98-99).

conventional lawn

conventional parking lot

LID lawn

LID parking lot

From Industrial to Low Impact Lawns

property

the industrial lawn
a linear train of inputs and wastestreams

the problem of over-fertilization
Suburban lawn care consumes more herbicides per acre than most farmers broadcast to grow crops.

maintenance
The average lawn consumes more than 10,000 gallons of water per summer, causing water shortages in not just arid parts of the country.

clippings
"One recent university study found that nitrogen fertilization could be replaced by a whopping 50% without the least effect in the quality of the turf so long as the clippings stayed put."

lawn care
Lawn care is a $40 billion a year industry—more than the GDP of Vietnam in 2003.

"...the lawn is one of America's leading crops."

*All information on these two pages from Ted Steinberg's *American Green: The Obsessive Quest for the Perfect Lawn*

the low impact lawn
a regenerative, closed loop system

productive lawn
An average sized lawn of around a third of an acre could produce enough vegetables to feed a family of six.

nutrient cycling
The bacteria necessary for nitrogenation of soil thrives in the polyculture of a low impact lawn; in the monoculture of industrial lawns the bacteria cannot survive.

compost
12.5% of refuse in landfills comes from food scraps while 12.8% comes from yard trimmings—this costly waste stream can be diverted and used for composting.

Botanizing
Lot and Lawn

property

turf pavers

pervious surfaces

enhance lawns and lots with
Rain gardens are an excellent
infiltration within existing
of low lying areas as natural
tolerate periods of extreme
addition to aesthetic benefits,
bioremediation—the removal
through plant processes.
can be transformed into
by cutting or removing curbs
stormwater runoff from

reduce impervious surfaces

Since impervious surfaces do not allow for infiltration of
stormwater, polluting substances that come into contact with
hard surfaces are concentrated and channelized during a
storm event, thus compounding polluted runoff dysfunctions.
Pervious surfaces increase on-site runoff infiltration and prevent
the transfer of pollution problems to another site. Pervious
surfaces should be used at the beginning of the treatment
network to slow and filter sediment before stormwater runoff
reaches secondary LID facilities for treatment. Pervious paving
is appropriate for parking zones and occasionally used drives,
but should be avoided in high traffic areas.

rain garden

"The average urban lawn could produce several hundred pounds of food a year."

LID treatment facilities

way to increase on-site lawns. They take advantage collection points for runoff and wetness and drought. In rain gardens facilitate and breakdown of pollutants For parking lots, tree islands stormwater treatment facilities and sinking islands to receive impervious surfaces.

xeriscape lawn

xeriscape landscape

central swale

remove high maintenance vegetation in favor of xeriscape

The industrialized lawn's lifecycle costs for irrigation, turf seed, chemical fertilizer, herbicides, fuel and equipment, and waste management of lawn clippings, are substantial, while their shallow root systems provide little infiltration or ecological services. On the other hand, xeriscape lawns have significant economic and environmental benefits, such as increased biodiversity, food production, on-site infiltration, and low maintenance. A multi-species mix of native grasses is already adapted to an area's climate and able to exist as a stable plant community. Native grass lawns provide the same appearance as non-native monocultures, and only require mowing every three to five weeks.

Lot Design

property

Property owners can implement varying degrees of LID on their lots.

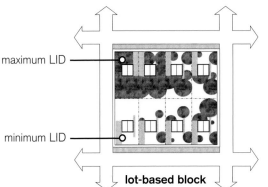

maximum LID

minimum LID

lot-based block

filtration

For property owners, one of the easiest ways to adapt LID to existing sites is by installing rain gardens in low lying areas. More holistic measures involve replacing existing lawns with native or local vegetation as well as replacing drives and walks with pervious paving. Before digging, however, make sure to contact a central agency or your local utility companies to locate all existing underground utilities.

For new construction, site planning should include measures that minimize impervious surfaces, protect ecologically sensitive areas of the site, and increase infiltration through the use of vegetation. Consider measures like reducing the length of driveways, limiting regrading of existing topography, minimizing building footprints, and protecting existing vegetation.

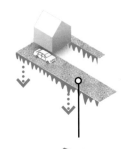

Slow

Use pervious paving for walks and drives. *Pervious Paving* pp. 172-173

One-third of all residential water use in the US is currently used for landscaping.

infiltration

treatment

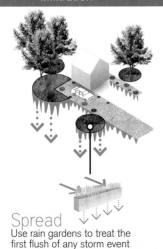

Spread
Use rain gardens to treat the first flush of any storm event and infiltrate runoff from **one to ten-year storm events**. *Rain Garden* pp. 178-179

Soak
Replace industrial lawn with xeriscape lawn to treat and infiltrate runoff from **one to twenty-five-year storm events**. Consult local nurseries or a landscape design professional for optimal seed mix and plants.

Block Design

property

Incorporate shared conservation areas into LID neighborhood fabrics by connecting property to easements.

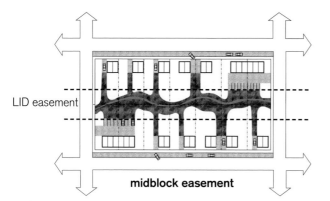

LID easement

midblock easement

When designing for LID at the block scale, several shared strategies can be implemented around an easement. The midblock easement connects individual parcels to a shared open space. This allows for conservation of existing habitat, pedestrian trails, and LID utility zones that bundle delivery of ecological services. Stormwater runoff from the house, driveway, and turf grass would enter the treatment system through a series of rain garden tributaries that extend to the shared LID easement. For redundancy and optimal networking, stormwater overflow from the street could be harbored in the midblock easement through connecting bioswales. The LID easement needs to be carefully coordinated with new and existing utility easements, which typically prohibit tree planting (see "Management, Not Maintenance" pp. 206-211).

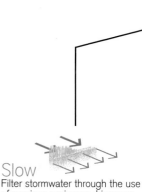

Slow
Filter stormwater through the use of pervious paving on driveways.
Pervious Paving pp. 172-173

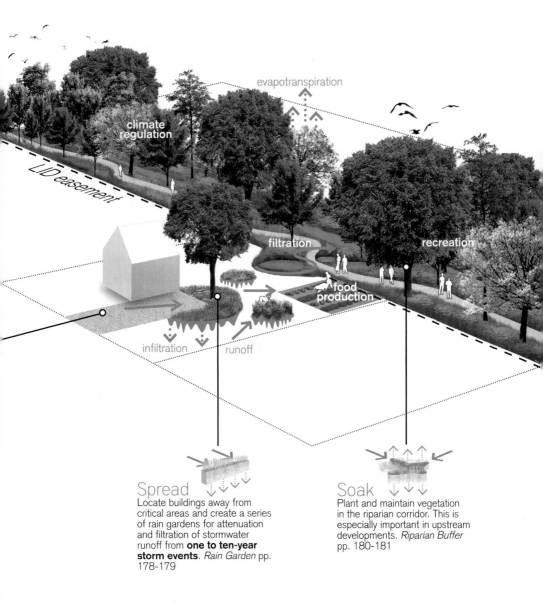

evapotranspiration

climate
regulation

LID easement

filtration

recreation

food
production

infiltration   runoff

Spread
Locate buildings away from
critical areas and create a series
of rain gardens for attenuation
and filtration of stormwater
runoff from **one to ten-year
storm events**. *Rain Garden* pp.
178-179

Soak
Plant and maintain vegetation
in the riparian corridor. This is
especially important in upstream
developments. *Riparian Buffer*
pp. 180-181

Block Design

property

Utilize a green alley in lieu of conventional alleys to combine the functions of access, parking, and stormwater management.

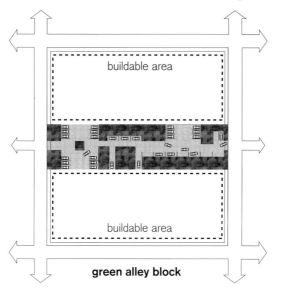

buildable area

buildable area

green alley block

habitat

erosion control

As existing access and utility corridors, urban alleys can be easily retrofitted to function as a LID utility. Due to low traffic flows, the alley could be resurfaced with pervious paving and lined with bioswales to allow for stormwater infiltration and treatment. As with any pervious surface, the alley should be kept clean of dirt and debris (see *The Chicago Green Alley Handbook*). Green alleys are vital alternatives to overburdened streets, improving the livability index of urban cores. New urban alleys require at least an 18 foot right-of-way with a 10 foot travel lane.

Slow
Use flush curbs to allow water to be distributed evenly over treatment facilities. *Flow Control Devices* pp. 148-149

evapotranspiration

filtration

treatment

infiltration

Spread

Reduce impervious surfaces to filter and attenuate stormwater from the street. *Pervious Paving* pp. 172-173

Soak

Apply rain gardens and bioswales in the easement for treatment during **one to ten-year storm events**. These facilities must be connected to secondary facilities to handle 10 to 50-year storm events. *Bioswale* pp. 182-183

Block Design

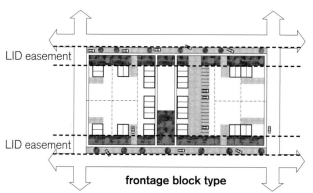 property

Employ LID easements along the street to create a connective fabric for stormwater management.

LID easement

LID easement

frontage block type

erosion control

Another block configuration creates LID easements at the front of the property in a treatment network of connected bioswales. Ideally, stormwater will first pass through a network of lot-based LID facilities, and use LID frontage facilities as overflow or secondary treatment. This allows the stormwater to slow and spread before it enters the conveyance system. The LID easement also receives stormwater runoff from the street if properly sized and designed. Runoff from the street should also be filtered before it enters the connected bioswales. This can be achieved through permeable paving and filter strips. These utility landscapes can radically improve neighborhood aesthetics and functioning.

Slow

Reduce impervious surfaces to attenuate stormwater from the street. *Pervious Paving* pp. 172-173

evapotranspiration

habitat

water
regulation

treatment

Spread
Use curb cuts to allow water to
distribute evenly into the swale.
Flow Control Devices pp. 148-
149

Soak
Create LID easements with
bioswales to treat and convey
water to larger LID facilities.
Bioswale pp. 182-183

Implementing LID in lawns
is so simple and effective...

...we already do it!

Surface Materials

property

porous asphalt
These pavements, used mostly for parking lots, allow water to drain through the pavement surface into a stone recharge bed and infiltrate into soils below the pavement.
- Heat Island Mitigation: Low
- Initial Cost: +10% above conventional
- Maintenance: Vacuum
- Durability: 10-30 years

pervious concrete
This pavement technology eliminates the need for retention ponds and other stormwater BMPs, lowering overall project costs.
- Heat Island Mitigation: Low to Moderate (depending on color)
- Initial Cost: +10% above conventional
- Maintenance: Vacuum
- Durability: 10-30 years

interlocking paver systems
Pre-cast concrete, natural stone, or brick units allow water to permeate around or through their surfaces.
- Heat Island Mitigation: Low to Moderate (depending on color)
- Initial Cost: High
- Maintenance: Vacuum
- Durability: 10-50 years

15 percent void space

When considering pervious paving, keep in mind that the voids of some systems require frequent vacuuming.

An impervious surface will generate two to six times more runoff than a natural surface.

alternative paving systems
One sustainable alternative material type is recycled rubber paving, which can be modular pavers or poured in place.
- Heat Island Mitigation: Moderate
- Initial Cost: Medium
- Maintenance: Vacuum
- Durability: 10-50 years

gravel systems
These systems consist of an injection molded ring and grid structure, underlain by geotextile fabric and a sandy gravel base course.
- Heat Island Mitigation: Moderate to High (depending on color)
- Initial Cost: Medium to High
- Maintenance: Add gravel
- Durability: 10-20 years

grass concrete and turf pavers
These systems provide significant load bearing strength while protecting vegetation root systems from compaction. Void spaces within the system allow excellent root development and water storage capacity.
- Heat Island Mitigation: High
- Initial Cost: High
- Maintenance: Watering
- Durability: 20-40 years

→ **90 percent void space**
Gravel and vegetated systems have larger void spaces, thus allowing for greater infiltration capacity. However, these systems will require occasional mowing and sediment removal.

Parking Lot Design

property

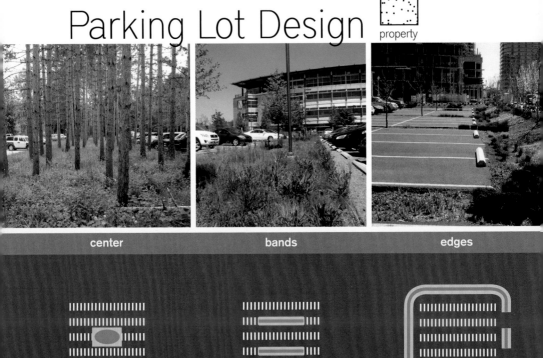

center   bands   edges

minimum level of ecological service

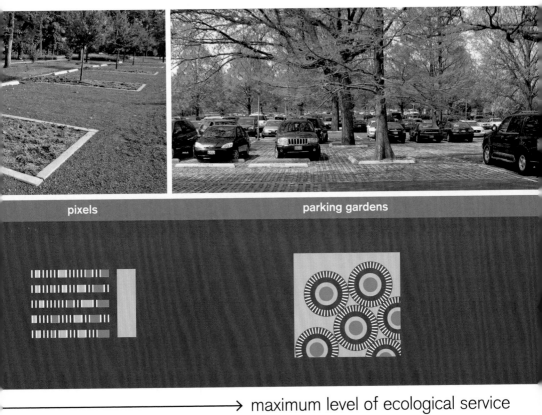

pixels

parking gardens

maximum level of ecological service

Pixelated Parking

property

Reduce impervious surfaces by pixelating the parking surface with LID paving and landscapes.

An intrinsically adaptive solution, ideal for retrofits, pixel configurations propose localized replacement of impervious surfaces with absorbent landscape islands and pervious paving. Recognizing that the outer 40 percent of many commercial parking lots are only used during peak demand twice a year, the lot frontage offers an excellent public garden without sacrificing parking capacity. The pixelated parking solution reduces stormwater runoff through the addition of trees and pervious paving, eliminating the need for conventional pipe-and-pond solutions.

Water from impervious drive aisles flows to the pervious parking stalls, slowing and redistributing runoff. Through curb cuts (see "Curb Alternatives" pp. 96-97), or flush curbs, the water is directed to vegetated islands, which are connected by a bioswale or underground oversized pipe. Peak flows eventually end in an overflow infiltration basin for groundwater recharge. If space is unavailable for an infiltration basin or other detention facility, stormwater can be detained in an underground storage facility for slow release into the municipal stormwater system.

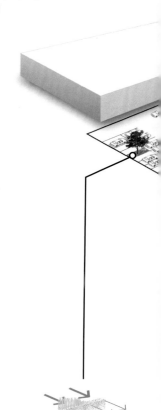

Slow

Remove curbs and sink tree islands in parking stalls to receive and filter stormwater from **one to ten-year storm events** as it enters treatment landscapes.
Bioswale pp. 182-183

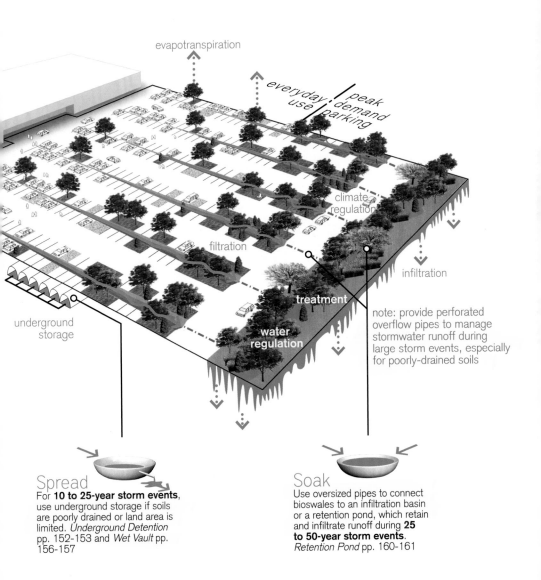

evapotranspiration

everyday use / peak demand parking

climate regulation

filtration

infiltration

treatment

water regulation

underground storage

note: provide perforated overflow pipes to manage stormwater runoff during large storm events, especially for poorly-drained soils

Spread
For **10 to 25-year storm events**, use underground storage if soils are poorly drained or land area is limited. *Underground Detention* pp. 152-153 and *Wet Vault* pp. 156-157

Soak
Use oversized pipes to connect bioswales to an infiltration basin or a retention pond, which retain and infiltrate runoff during **25 to 50-year storm events**. *Retention Pond* pp. 160-161

atmospheric regulation

flow attenuation

soil formation
infiltration
erosion control

climate regulation

Heifer International
Little Rock, Arkansas

filtration
sediment retention
flow attenuation

Parking Gardens

property

Reconfigure conventional parking lot models to serve the hydrology of the site, where cars sit in their own treatment basins.

There is no reason for parking lots to be so ugly, costly, and of low ecological performance. They are simple land uses with equal effectiveness in a variety of configurations. Rather than conceive of the lot as a storage space, think of the parking lot as a stormwater garden with landscape architectural features. In the illustrated case, parking garden configurations propose a set of tangent LID landscape modules that function as a treatment network while larger green spaces at the outer areas serve as percolation parks for larger storm events. As with pixelated parking configurations, stormwater runoff begins in the drive aisle. Each parking garden is sloped toward the center allowing runoff conveyance over pervious paving into the rain garden. Rain gardens are connected to infiltration basins by underground perforated pipe to handle overflow from larger storm events. This is the most efficient configuration, as the car sits in its own treatment facility, minimizing runoff conveyance to remote facilities.

Slow

Construct rain gardens in center of parking modules to treat first flush and infiltrate most contaminated runoff during **one to ten-year storm events**. *Rain Garden* pp. 178-179

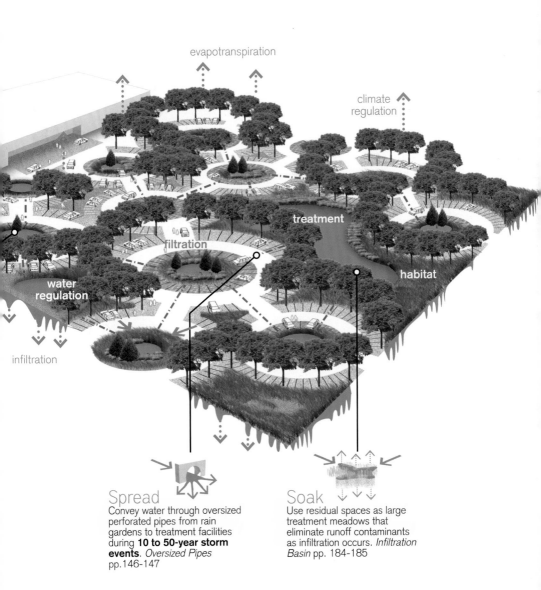

evapotranspiration

climate
regulation

treatment

filtration

habitat

water
regulation

infiltration

Spread
Convey water through oversized
perforated pipes from rain
gardens to treatment facilities
during **10 to 50-year storm
events**. *Oversized Pipes*
pp.146-147

Soak
Use residual spaces as large
treatment meadows that
eliminate runoff contaminants
as infiltration occurs. *Infiltration
Basin* pp. 184-185

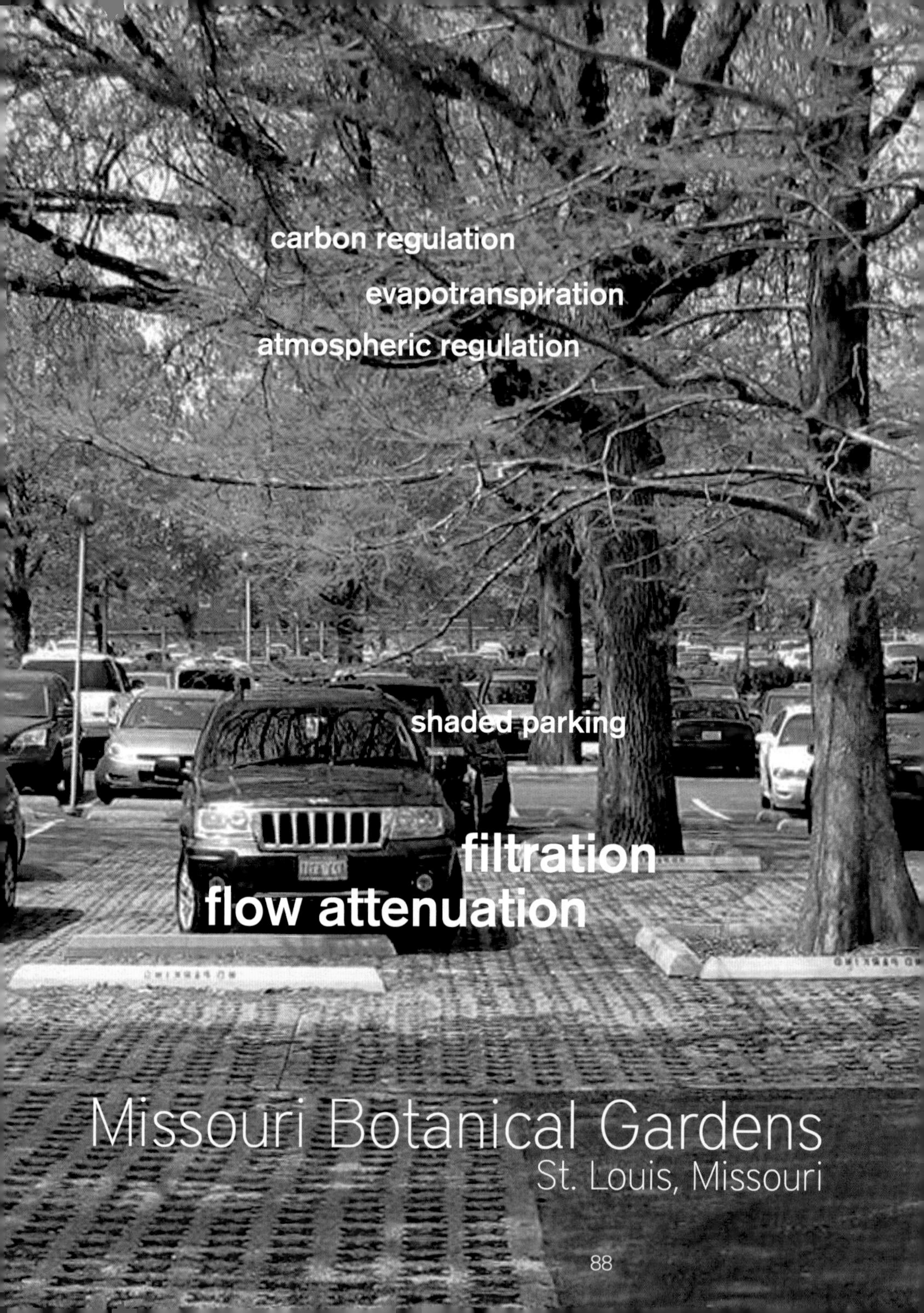

carbon regulation

evapotranspiration

atmospheric regulation

shaded parking

filtration

flow attenuation

Missouri Botanical Gardens
St. Louis, Missouri

heat island mitigation

climate regulation

sediment retention
infiltration
erosion control

conventional
drain, direct, dispatch

street

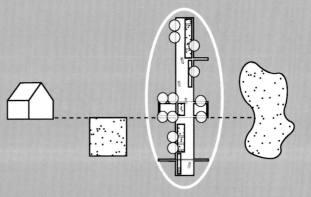

low impact
slow, spread, soak

LID
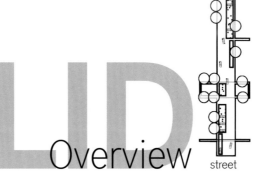
Overview
street

Streets occupy 25 percent of our urban landscape and are key to LID implementation. However, since street design was professionalized by civil engineers in the 1920s, two basic urban services have dominated street design criteria—maximization of vehicle flow per lane per hour and drainage. LID supports the return of urban services (i.e., gathering, play, commerce, and relaxation) that were once offered by streets and their public right-of-ways. Differing from the traditional street, LID streets introduce facilities that deliver a full spectrum of ecological services. Keep in mind that the public right-of-way includes the street, sidewalk, bike paths, utilities, stormwater management infrastructure, and landscape systems.

Like smart buildings, streets can be designed to function ecologically, amplifying wise natural resource use rather than becoming another liability. LID streets, or green streets, are context-sensitive, designed to accommodate multiple transit modes, ensure pedestrian and bicycle safety, enhance sociability, and provide ecologically-based stormwater management. LID stormwater management goals for the right-of-way include minimization of impervious pavement and maximization of landscaped spaces. This may entail design of new street geometries like the Dutch-inspired "shared street", a street type essentially configured to function like a series of public gardens rather than a strict traffic corridor.

In designing green streets it is important to coordinate utility infrastructure for easy access and management (see "Management, Not Maintenance" pp. 206-211). Utilities should not be located within LID stormwater facilities to prevent damage to vegetation when utility access is required.

How can we transform the **street right-of-way**?

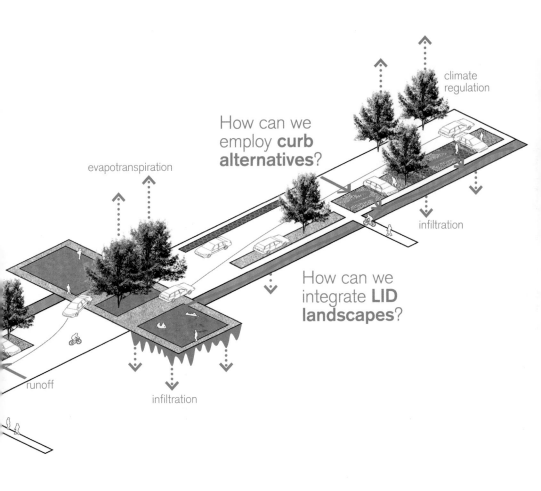

climate
regulation

evapotranspiration

How can we
employ **curb
alternatives**?

infiltration

How can we
integrate **LID
landscapes**?

runoff

infiltration

Components of
Low Impact Streets

street

curb cuts

flush curbs

soft infrastructure
The flow rate of stormwater before it enters the can accomplish this through attenuate and filter water for street edge, LID facilities which house new rain space, reduce flow rates stormwater runoff.

curb alternatives
Conventional urban streets employ curbs to channel stormwater runoff to catch basins where untreated water is dispatched to another location. LID curb alternatives evenly redistribute runoff to adjacent treatment facilities, retaining as much stormwater on site as possible. This is achieved by cutting curbs or eliminating them altogether. Curb choice depends on land use and stormwater volume to be managed. Curbs can be used as a safety feature in high traffic areas to separate pedestrians from vehicles.

pervious parking

runoff should be reduced treatment network. Streets pervious paving systems that sediment removal. At the such as curb extensions, gardens in reclaimed street by treating and infiltrating

bioswale   rain garden

LID curb extensions

plants, not pipes

LID replaces pipe-and-pond systems with facultative planting — or a community of wetland plants — to metabolize pollutants in stormwater runoff. Instead of transporting polluted stormwater elsewhere, LID planting attenuates and treats water on site, allowing for retention and infiltration. Other benefits include mitigation of the heat island effect, cost savings for treatment, and preservation of water quality.

Curb Alternatives

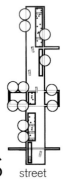 street

perforated pre-cast curbs
Perforated pre-cast curbs can be installed in new developments to allow water flow.
- Sediment Capture: Low
- Traffic Level: Moderate/High
- Maintenance: High

pre-fabricated curb inserts
These inserts can be used in a retrofit of an existing curb or new construction, while maintaining the curb's structural integrity. Water energy-dissipating measures are not necessary to prevent erosion if the inlets are close together.
- Sediment Capture: Low
- Traffic Level: Moderate/High
- Maintenance: High

curb cut
Curbs can be cut in a retrofit or new construction. Curb cuts can vary in length, allowing for greater flow control.
- Sediment Capture: Low
- Traffic Level: Moderate
- Maintenance: Moderate

from point source flow —————————

flush curb
A flush curb maximizes uniform distribution of water from the street to the treatment facility. When used with a shallow, half inch lip, water can pond, allowing sediment to settle for eventual removal by street sweepers.
• Sediment Capture: Low
• Traffic Level: Moderate/Low
• Maintenance: Low

paving strip with sediment trench
Pervious pavers can filter sediment from street runoff, and serve as a tactile warning for straying automobiles.
• Sediment Capture: Moderate
• Traffic Level: Moderate/Low
• Maintenance: Low

double flush curb with sediment trench
An aggregate trench between flush curbs captures sediment, keeping it out of the treatment facility.
• Sediment Capture: High
• Traffic Level: Low
• Maintenance: High

*All information on these two pages from Metro Portland's *Green Streets: Innovative Solutions for Stormwater and Stream Crossings*

→ to distributed sheet flow

Designing for Urban Trees

street

Streets should be designed to accommodate tree root growth—the most critical factor in implementing tree lined streets.

Healthy trees are essential components of green infrastructure and urban forestry. Shade trees planted along hard surfaces reduce the heat island effect and improve air quality. Besides functioning as carbon sinks, trees also reduce stormwater runoff through interception, evapotranspiration, throughfall, and flow attenuation. Trees help create a sense of place, reduce noise and glare, and provide a safety barrier for pedestrians from traffic, which is why neighborhood value is increased by their presence.

Trees vary in their growth requirements and rates based on the biological and physical conditions of the site. Trees should be chosen based on cold hardiness, mature size and shape, drought tolerance, rooting characteristics, and resistance to insect and disease problems. For a list of suitable urban trees, consult a local nursery or landscape design professional (also see "Urban Trees for Zones 4-8" pp. 100-101).

The planting area should accommodate the anticipated root structure at maturity, ensuring absorption of water and nutrients. Remember that roots can extend well beyond the canopy of the tree. Use structural soil for adequate root penetration while minimizing damage to paved surfaces. Spacing between trees should reflect species' crown size at maturity. With proper planning and care, urban street trees can live well beyond their average 10-year lifespan.

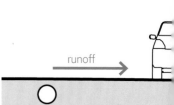

runoff

utilities: Locate underground utilities away from root systems. Trenching can cause irreparable damage to roots. Employ tunneling or trenchless technologies to promote non-destructive installation and inspection of utility infrastructure.

Due to soil compaction and poor planning the average lifespan of an urban tree is less than 10 years according to the USDA Forest Service.

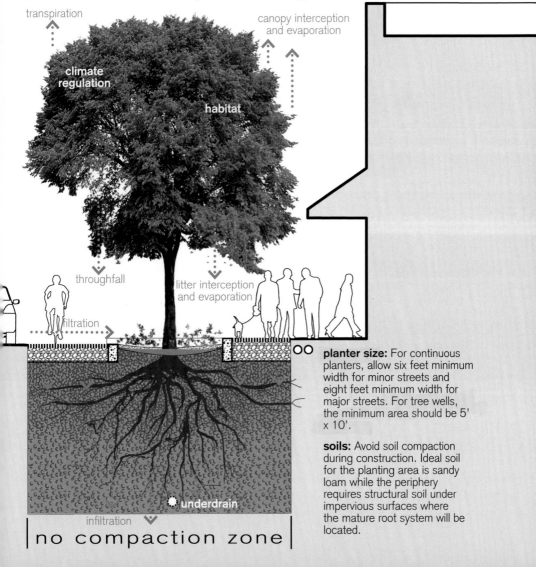

transpiration

canopy interception and evaporation

climate regulation

habitat

throughfall

litter interception and evaporation

filtration

planter size: For continuous planters, allow six feet minimum width for minor streets and eight feet minimum width for major streets. For tree wells, the minimum area should be 5' x 10'.

soils: Avoid soil compaction during construction. Ideal soil for the planting area is sandy loam while the periphery requires structural soil under impervious surfaces where the mature root system will be located.

underdrain

infiltration

no compaction zone

Urban Trees for Zones 4-8

street

chinese pistache

eastern redbud

ginkgo

common name	scientific name	mature sizing	spacing	growth rate
American Hornbeam	*Ostrya virginiana*	25-35'	20'	slow
Amur Maple	*Acer ginnala*	15-20'	15'	moderate
Chinese Pistache	*Pistacia chinensis*	20-30'	20'	moderate-fast
Dawn Redwood	*Metasequoia glyptostroboides*	65'	25'	moderate-fast
Eastern Redbud	*Cercis canadensis*	20-30'	20'	moderate
Fringetree	*Chionanthus virginicus*	15-25'	15'	slow
Ginkgo	*Ginkgo biloba*	60-75'	30'	slow
Littleleaf Linden	*Tilia cordata*	60-70'	25'	moderate
'Green Vase' Zelkova	*Zelkova serrata*	70'	40'	moderate-fast
Kentucky Coffee Tree	*Gymnocladus dioicus*	40-60'	40'	moderate
Lacebark Elm	*Ulmus parvifolia*	40-50'	40'	moderate
Cherokee™ Sweetgum	*Liquidamber styraciflua*	60-75'	40'	moderate-fast
Red Oak	*Querus rubra*	60-75'	50'	fast
Shagbark Hickory	*Carya ovata*	70-80'	30'	moderate
Willow Oak	*Querus phellos*	40-60'	40'	moderate

To traffic engineers, a tree is known as an FHO—Fixed and Hazardous Object.

'green vase' zelkova

lacebark elm

red oak

hardiness zone	notes
3 - 9	tolerates poor soils, seed clusters resemble hops
3 - 8	tolerant of urban conditions, multi-stemmed, utility friendly, will grow in planters
6 - 9	drought tolerant, red fall color
5 - 8	prefers moist soils, small leaf litter
4 - 9	adaptable to most soils except soggy sites, utility friendly, pink flowers
4 - 9	full sun, tolerates urban conditions, utility friendly, showy white flowers
4 - 8	tolerant of urban conditions, gold fall color, plant only male
3 - 7	tolerant of pollution, fragrant flower
5 - 8	very adaptable and disease resistant
3 - 8	tolerates drought and urban conditions
5 - 9	resistant to Dutch Elm disease, beautiful bark
5 - 9	grows on most sites, great fall color, plant fruitless selections
3 - 7	tolerant of urban conditions, red fall color
4 - 8	moist, well drained soils, golden brown fall color, interesting bark
5 - 9	adaptable to most soils, small leaf litter

zone 4

5

6

7

8

Street Types

street

skinny streets　　　　　**green streets**　　　　　**shared streets**

from local streets ————————————————————

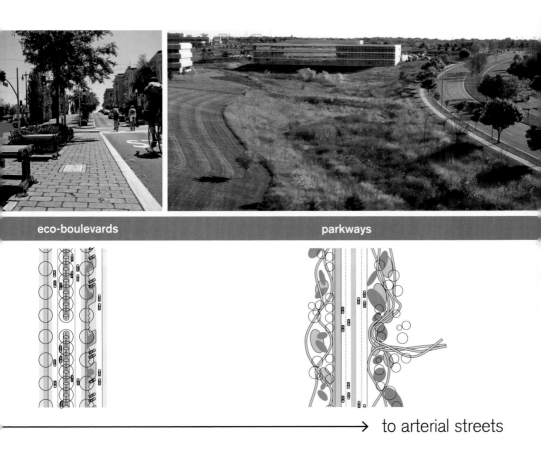

eco-boulevards

parkways

→ to arterial streets

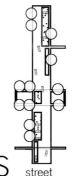

Skinny Streets

Create narrower streets to reduce runoff loading and substitute pervious paving for impervious surfaces to encourage stormwater infiltration.

Residential street design standards dating back to the 1960s called for local street widths as high as 36 feet. Miles of American streets have been designed and built to these standards, which are now recognized as unsafe, and an unwise use of fossil fuel-based resources. Wide streets generate large stormwater runoff peak loads due to their extensive impervious surface area. Since the 1990s, many cities have revisited their street design standards, subsequently adopting narrower street profiles, some as narrow as 20 feet wide for low traffic volumes, while still accommodating emergency vehicle access.

Reducing the width of streets provides a number of benefits. While many may initially assume they are unsafe, these narrow roads, or "skinny streets" actually reduce average speeds and vehicle accident rates. For instance, a 24-foot wide street has about 0.32 accidents per mile per year, while a 36 foot wide street has 1.21 (Walker Macy - *Villebois* v.4). Economic benefits include reduced street maintenance and resurfacing costs, while environmental benefits include reduced urban heat island effect. Soft-engineered streets provide stormwater runoff attenuation and filtering. However, such facilities handle only one to two-year storm events, requiring connection to a treatment network for larger events.

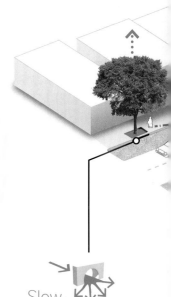

Slow

Cut curbs to allow for stormwater flow into curb extensions or other LID facilities. *Flow Control Devices* pp. 148-149

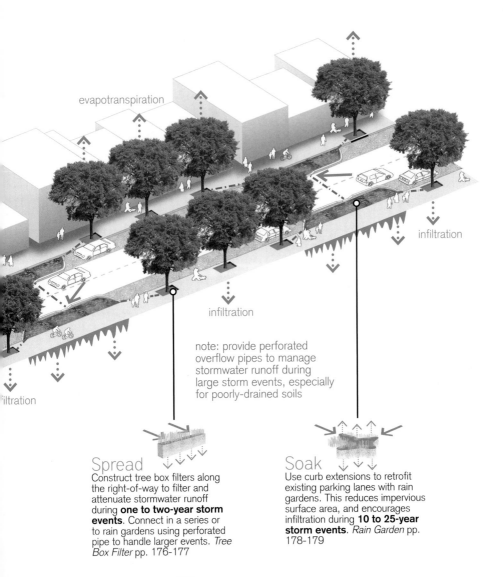

evapotranspiration

infiltration

infiltration

infiltration

note: provide perforated
overflow pipes to manage
stormwater runoff during
large storm events, especially
for poorly-drained soils

Spread
Construct tree box filters along
the right-of-way to filter and
attenuate stormwater runoff
during **one to two-year storm
events**. Connect in a series or
to rain gardens using perforated
pipe to handle larger events. *Tree
Box Filter* pp. 176-177

Soak
Use curb extensions to retrofit
existing parking lanes with rain
gardens. This reduces impervious
surface area, and encourages
infiltration during **10 to 25-year
storm events**. *Rain Garden* pp.
178-179

Siskiyou Street
Portland, Oregon

heat island mitigation

curb extension

infiltration

non-invasive facultative landscapes

erosion control and
sediment retention

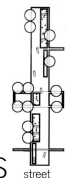
street

Shared Streets

*Design local streets as landscapes that balance the
social needs of pedestrians, transit, and stormwater
management.*

Shared streets, or "livable streets", are public spaces that
allow vehicles, pedestrians and bicyclists to safely share
the street without the conventional mode separators like
lanes, sidewalks, and curbs. Shared streets are designed
as multipurpose landscapes that calm vehicular traffic.
They provide LID management functions, and reclaim
social functions lost to the automobile's dominance.
Modeled after the Dutch "living street" or *woonerf*, shared
streets have a remarkable record of safety where they
have been implemented. Instead of investing in standard
traffic calming devices such as speed bumps, humps,
and regulating signs, the shared street employs varied
street geometries that compress the optical width of the
throughway. The uncertainty and intrigue intrinsic to the
spatial structure of the shared street becomes a "mental
speed bump", which naturally slows motorist speed.

While they deliver numerous social services (i.e., recreation,
crime prevention, traffic calming, and conviviality), shared
streets are ideal LID treatment facilities. The uniquely
integral public right-of-way configurations in shared
streets allow for a full range of water management
functions throughout the streetscape. Since curbs are
eliminated per design, parking stalls (and in some cases
drive aisles) can be constructed of pervious paving, and
open areas can be used as constructed wetlands to filter
and infiltrate stormwater runoff. Distributed facilities
should be connected with oversized or perforated pipe
to create redundancy and sized according to the amount

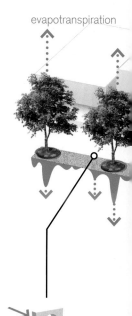

evapotranspiration

Slow

Instead of creating channelized
flow, remove curbs to allow sheet
flow, which reduces the velocity
of runoff. *Flow Control Devices*
pp. 148-149

108

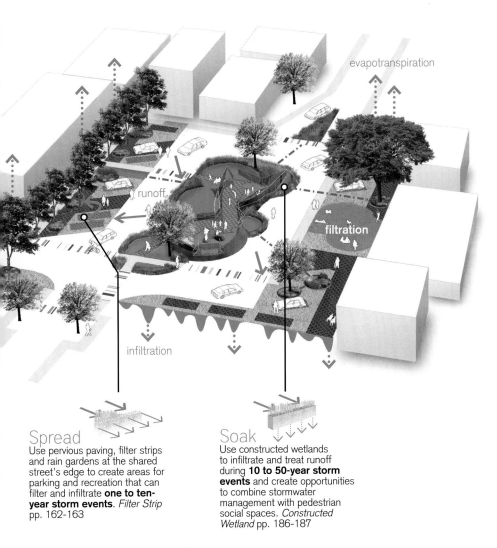

evapotranspiration

runoff

filtration

infiltration

Spread
Use pervious paving, filter strips and rain gardens at the shared street's edge to create areas for parking and recreation that can filter and infiltrate **one to ten-year storm events**. *Filter Strip* pp. 162-163

Soak
Use constructed wetlands to infiltrate and treat runoff during **10 to 50-year storm events** and create opportunities to combine stormwater management with pedestrian social spaces. *Constructed Wetland* pp. 186-187

of stormwater runoff expected to enter the street. Stormwater runoff can also be harvested and stored underground for later use.

Shared streets are typically implemented in residential areas with low traffic volumes. Though superior living environments, they are an uncommon street typology in America, with the closest concept being a town square, plaza, or pedestrian promenade that artfully accommodates all modes of transportation. Due to the shared street's unique street geometries and use of vegetation in the public right-of-way, city code variances may be required (see "Policies, Codes, and Covenants" pp. 196-205).

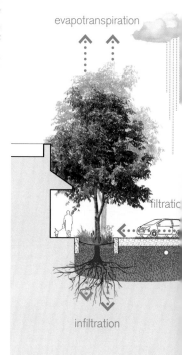

evapotranspiration

filtratic

infiltration

sidewalk | bioswale | pervious parking

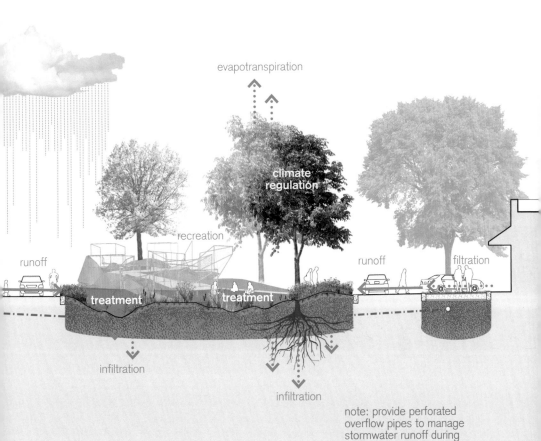

evapotranspiration

climate regulation

recreation

runoff

treatment

treatment

runoff

filtration

infiltration

infiltration

note: provide perforated overflow pipes to manage stormwater runoff during large storm events, especially for poorly-drained soils

street|constructed wetland|street|pervious parking

heat island mitigation

climate regulation

infiltration

rain garden

flush curbs

shared throughway
(single ground surface)

Willamette Street
Eugene, Oregon

parallel parking

rain garden

infiltration

flush curbs

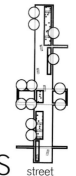
street

Eco-Boulevards

Create streets with green medians that also deliver water treatment services.

The word "boulevard" originated in France, and describes an elegantly wide road that uses vegetated medians to separate arterial throughways from the slower pace of local streets. The median strip slows travel, buffers against oncoming traffic, and provides vegetation that shades the road. The street promotes walking by providing a safe, appealing, and comfortable social environment. An eco-boulevard enhances this street typology by utilizing medians for stormwater management and networking to open spaces throughout the district.

Eco-boulevards utilize long strips of the public right-of-way, transforming them into green infrastructure. Stormwater runoff flows across the impervious road surface towards the edge of the eco-boulevard and enters vegetated medians through designated curbing strategies (see "Curb Alternatives" pp. 96-97), the latter of which may include the removal of raised curbs. The median is depressed and converted into a bioswale, allowing for drainage and infiltration. To attenuate flow, the median is divided by check dams or tree mounds. To handle larger storm events, the eco-boulevard can be connected to conventional stormwater systems or to open space greenways for stormwater conveyance. Features typically found in the eco-boulevard include bike lanes and wide sidewalks. Bike lanes are located adjacent to the street when used for commuting, and separated by a vegetated strip when used for recreation. While eco-boulevards should be designed with narrower street widths (11-foot travel lanes) than traditional boulevards, they are generally associated with a high amount of impervious

Slow

Use tree mounds or check dams in medians to attenuate and detain runoff, allowing stormwater a chance to infiltrate during **one to ten-year storm events**. *Flow Control Devices* pp. 148-149

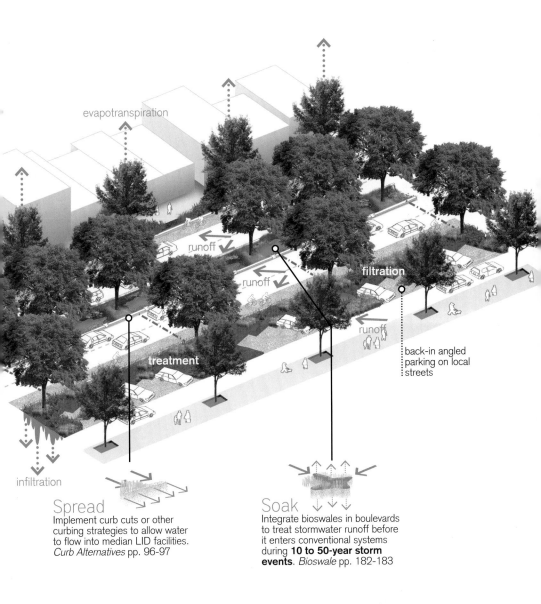

evapotranspiration

runoff

runoff

filtration

runoff

treatment

back-in angled
parking on local
streets

infiltration

Spread
Implement curb cuts or other
curbing strategies to allow water
to flow into median LID facilities.
Curb Alternatives pp. 96-97

Soak
Integrate bioswales in boulevards
to treat stormwater runoff before
it enters conventional systems
during **10 to 50-year storm
events**. *Bioswale* pp. 182-183

surface area. Larger capacity stormwater facilities should be used to compensate for the larger amount of runoff.

Eco-boulevards are located in intensely developed areas with active pedestrian activity. Eco-boulevards should be engineered for low speeds through the use of narrow lanes and on-street parking. Sidewalks should be well lit and clear of obstructions. One obstacle to eco-boulevards is the prohibition of LID stormwater facilities in the public right-of-way by city code, requiring a variance or amendment (see "Policies, Codes, and Covenants" pp. 196-205). Utilities should be located outside of LID stormwater facilities to prevent the vegetation from being damaged when access to utilities is required. Digging up LID facilities would compromise stormwater management performance if there is not enough system redundancy. Instead, utilities can be placed under sidewalks or streets as city codes allow.

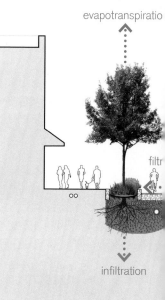

evapotranspiratio

filtr

infiltration

sidewalk | filter strip | pervious bicycle lane

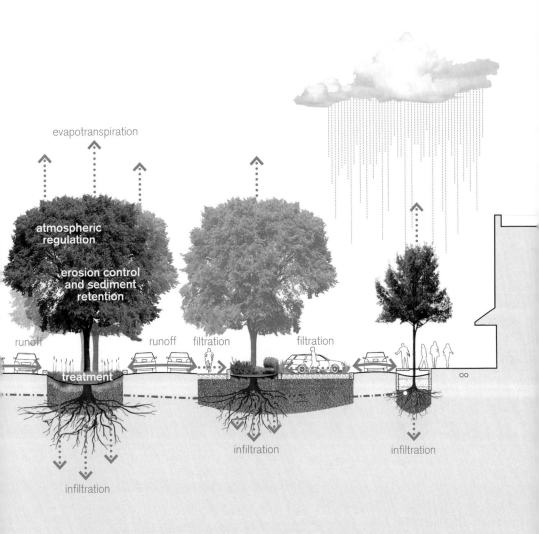

evapotranspiration

atmospheric
regulation

erosion control
and sediment
retention

runoff   runoff   filtration   filtration

treatment

infiltration   infiltration   infiltration

infiltration

central | stormwater | central | pervious | bioswale | pervious | local | tree box | sidewalk
arterial | median | arterial | bicycle lane | | parking | street | filter |

117

central arterial

rain garden

Octavia Boulevard
San Francisco, California

heat island mitigation

atmospheric regulation

shared local street

shaded sidewalk

pervious paving

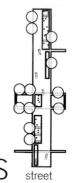

Parkways street

Improve the street right-of-way akin to a greenway landscape.

Parkways integrate multiple civic functions into an existing arterial highway landscape, creating a unique transportation system with environmental, social, and architectural functions. Combining the services offered by pedestrian-oriented greenways and trails with the highway, this category of thoroughfare accommodates different transit modes and their intrinsic speeds. Parkways connect regional and local interests, optimizing transportation quality through parks and green infrastructure.

In addition to pedestrian facilities, the parkway also includes LID treatment facilities. LID facilities utilized in parkways offer ecological services not available in a conventional roadway, such as habitat protection, conservation buffers, and flood retention. As a result of the larger right-of-way, parkways can handle one to two-year storm events as well as larger 25 to 50-year events. Parkways provide a unique urban landscape at regional scales, requiring integrated government administration and regulation.

Slow

Use a level spreader to transform concentrated stormwater runoff into sheet flow for distribution over a filter strip. *Flow Control Devices* pp. 148-149

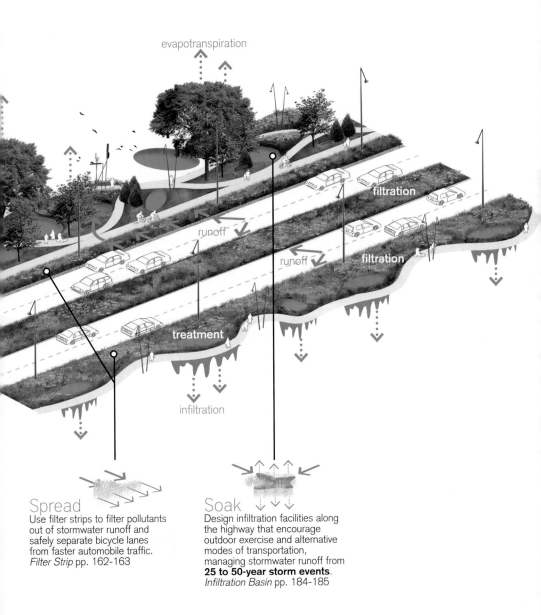

evapotranspiration

filtration

filtration

runoff

runoff

treatment

infiltration

Spread
Use filter strips to filter pollutants out of stormwater runoff and safely separate bicycle lanes from faster automobile traffic.
Filter Strip pp. 162-163

Soak
Design infiltration facilities along the highway that encourage outdoor exercise and alternative modes of transportation, managing stormwater runoff from **25 to 50-year storm events**.
Infiltration Basin pp. 184-185

heat island mitigation

flow attenuation

Eastern Parkway
Louisville, Kentucky

climate regulation

evapotranspiration

refugia/habitat

recreation

filter strip

infiltration

open

conventional
drain, direct, dispatch

space

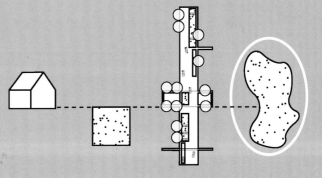

low impact
slow, spread, soak

LID Overview

open space

Urban green space, or open space, consists of publicly regulated land areas and waterbodies that conserve and shape the urban environment. Currently, open spaces offer recreational, aesthetic, and ecological functions, however with planning, they can deliver more comprehensive ecological services. Vegetated open space at the scale of the city and region can deliver vital ecological services not feasible at the scale of the lot, block, or neighborhood. To achieve this, open space should be comprehensively planned as a green network that maintains waterbody functioning and ecosystem connectivity through the use of designed parks, greenways, and self-organizing conservation areas. Studies in multiple disciplines, from public health to economics and transportation planning, are finding that well-planned urban open space systems yield compounding economic, environmental, and social returns far beyond expectations that motivated initial project investments.

How can
we develop
to ensure
conservation?

The first recognized interconnected urban open space system in North America was Boston's Emerald Necklace designed by Frederick Law Olmsted between 1878 and 1890 (on right pp. 124-125). This green network recognized the need for a large system to mitigate urban flooding and water pollution while serving civic and recreational needs. While other plans soon followed by similarly minded cities and their landscape architects, by the 1930s growing investments in highway infrastructure redirected attention away from urban open space development. Programs and policies recommending greenways did not emerge again until 1985 when the President's Commission on Americans Outdoors emphasized the value of interconnected greenways through a proposed national greenway network to connect cities.

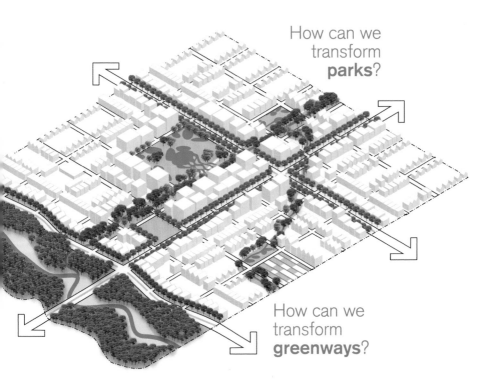

How can we
transform
parks?

How can we
transform
greenways?

Conventional versus LID Urbanism

Since planning has to work within a market-driven development framework, where open space is a placeholder for future development, many agencies have not developed a regional or local open space plan. Such a plan would coordinate the conservation of open space in the public interest. This includes riparian systems, floodplains, sensitive ecological areas, forested preserves, heritage farmlands, street right-of-ways, and park and trail systems. Rather than preserve isolated bits of greenery, LID urbanism, through various incentives and conservation trust funding, creates urban and regional connectivity that balances competing demands between open space and urban land use interests.

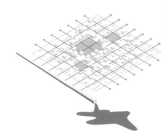

conventional urbanism
drain, direct, dispatch

LID provides opportunities to reconnect with nature. Urban open space can help overcome the "nature deficit disorder" articulated by Richard Louv in his acclaimed book, *Last Child in the Woods*. Louv chronicles a wide range of behavioral disorders now experienced by younger generations who lack any meaningful exposure to, and literacy of, the natural environment.

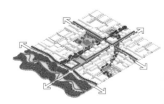

LID urbanism
slow, spread, soak

Ecology at the Scale of City and Region

A declension of open spaces integrated with the urban environment is fundamental to a watershed approach in urban development. Besides filtering and treatment, open space at the scale of the city supports a regional watershed's ability to recharge the aquifer and groundwater for maintenance of stream base flows. Open space connectivity is crucial for maintaining wildlife habitat and migration corridors, which support urban biodiversity and ecosystem resiliency. Some climax mammalian species familiar to urban areas require over 50 square miles per adult. Most importantly, healthy open space networks house robust local genetic pools, sustaining ecosystem development and maturity.

Ecological services delivered at regional scales include wetland protection vital to flood control because wetlands function as reserve storage during prolonged periods of peak flow. Wetlands, wet meadows, and waterbody buffers also reduce the risk from unregulated urban contaminants and toxic spills that may reach streams and lakes, particularly those used for drinking water supplies. Indeed, conservation functioning in forested open space exponentially reduces contamination risks to water supplies, reducing water treatment costs. A study released by The Trust for Public Land, showing the relationship between treatment costs and forest cover, revealed that for every 10 percent increase in forest cover, treatment and chemical costs decreased by approximately 20 percent (www.tpl.org).

Conservation Planning

One of the biggest contributors to contemporary ecological dysfunction is sprawling urban development. Urban sprawl has led to habitat loss, fragmentation, and loss of invaluable ecological biodiversity. Possibly the highest aspiration that cities and regions can aim for is to halt destruction of existing habitat and plan for a system of interconnected greenways that restores damaged ecological structure. Since ecosystems typically exceed legal boundaries, cumulative land-use decisions at the local level adversely impact watersheds at a regional scale. Every polluting input at the local level has a compounding effect on urban runoff. Negative impacts culminate in unhealthy stream flow regimes marked by flash flooding, altered stream morphologies, elevated nutrient and contaminant levels, excessive sedimentation from eroded stream banks, and loss of species diversity. Therefore, local decisions play a significant role in the conservation of biodiversity, and thus the need for the watershed approach at local scales of development.

Conservation Development

open space

Preserve native vegetation, sensitive ecological habitat, and open space by using conservation development techniques.

Conservation of open space and clustered development mutually underpin the watershed approach. Compact residential development conserves 30-80 percent of a site's buildable land as permanent, undivided open space. This contrasts with conventional development where the site is subdivided and parceled out to property owners, regardless of ecological structure. While lots in conventional neighborhoods may be large, their natural landscapes are usually replaced by industrial lawns that diminish ecological functioning. Despite their low densities, sprawling subdivisions ruin viewsheds that initially attracted property investors to the site.

conventional development

Conservation design deeds primary conservation areas, such as wetlands, waterbodies, floodplains, and steep slopes, to a public or quasi-public interest. Secondary conservation areas such as prime agricultural land, forested areas, critical ecological habitat areas and upland buffers should also be considered for preservation. Subsequent steps include siting houses, roads, and trails in clustered configurations without sacrificing privacy. Conservation design allows for the same number of homes as a conventional development, with greater savings in infrastructure costs due to shorter street lengths (local roads cost $300-600 per linear foot). As numerous real estate studies have shown, increased density and shared open space also offer spatial unity and ecological integrity while creating premium market value.

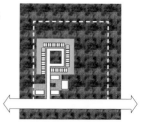

conservation development

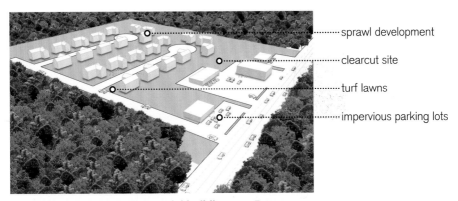

····· sprawl development

····· clearcut site

····· turf lawns

····· impervious parking lots

25 houses and 4 commercial buildings on 5 acres

····· shared open space

····· clustered development

····· preserved trees

····· pervious pavement

25 houses and 4 commercial buildings on 5 acres

Treatment Parks

open space

Introduce stormwater management as another ecological service delivered by urban parks.

Public parks are typically conceived as places for passive or active recreation. When people consider sustainable development they usually think of buildings. Yet, parks can readily integrate recreation with stormwater management, resulting in improved environmental performance, greater community benefits, and reduced maintenance costs. While it is easier to implement LID facilities in new developments, opportunities are available for retrofitting existing developments as well. An emerging trend for retrofitting existing urban infrastructure involves the incorporation of stormwater treatment parks

Like all LID landscapes, parks should be considered as interdependent and interconnected spaces that share systems of soil, water, vegetation, and topography. A treatment park can use demonstration LID design solutions to reveal and celebrate natural processes that slow, spread and soak stormwater. Treatment parks are designed to filter stormwater from surrounding public streets, which is currently being piped and transferred to another site or treatment plant. Stormwater treatment becomes an asset instead of a liability, didactically teaching the community about ecological stewardship in managing the urban environment.

Community participation in park planning is important to encourage public ownership and stewardship beyond public agency management. Good open space design with multiple functions will contribute to the adoption of LID practices if they are appreciated and sponsored by the surrounding community.

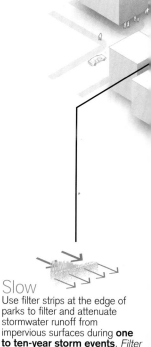

Slow
Use filter strips at the edge of parks to filter and attenuate stormwater runoff from impervious surfaces during **one to ten-year storm events**. *Filter Strip* pp. 162-163

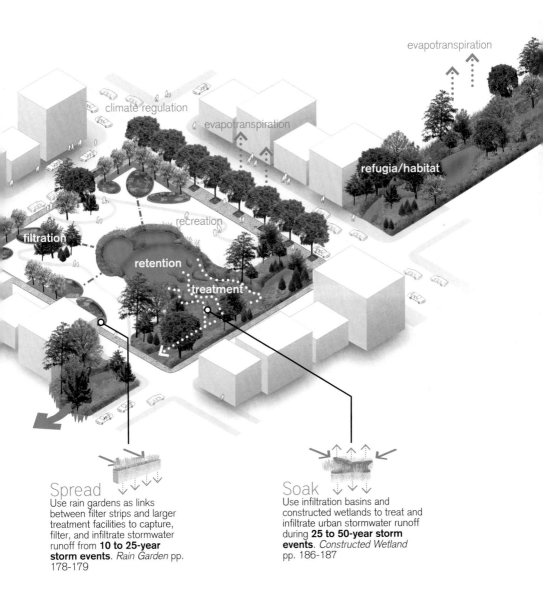

evapotranspiration

climate regulation

evapotranspiration

refugia/habitat

recreation

filtration

retention

treatment

Spread
Use rain gardens as links between filter strips and larger treatment facilities to capture, filter, and infiltrate stormwater runoff from **10 to 25-year storm events**. *Rain Garden* pp. 178-179

Soak
Use infiltration basins and constructed wetlands to treat and infiltrate urban stormwater runoff during **25 to 50-year storm events**. *Constructed Wetland* pp. 186-187

Water Harvesting Parks

open space

Recycle stormwater runoff as irrigation for high maintenance parks, such as community gardens and sports fields.

Harvesting rainwater is not a new concept, just a forgotten one. Before the advent of centralized municipal water supply systems, communities relied on rainwater harvesting as a source for household, landscape, and agricultural water needs. Rainwater was collected from roofs and stored on site in cisterns. The proliferation of centralized, reliable water treatment and distribution systems in urban areas has displaced rainwater harvesting practices. However, a renewed interest in wise resource use has emerged in response to the rising energy cost of moving water around. Water scarcities are occurring even in traditionally water-rich regions like those in Florida and around the Great Lakes.

While it would be ecologically ideal for all parks to contain native, low maintenance vegetation that can treat urban runoff, this may not always be practical. Large areas for organized sports and local food production require significant irrigation in order to maintain vegetation. Instead of using costly potable water as the source for this irrigation, rainwater harvesting offers a sustainable alternative. Water from surrounding impervious surfaces can be collected in a treatment network, filtered and stored. For land uses involving food production, harvested stormwater runoff must be thoroughly treated. When the water is needed, a wind driven or motorized pump can be used to draw it from storage for distribution through an irrigation system.

Slow ↓ ↓ ↓

Use bioswales to capture and filter stormwater runoff from impervious surfaces during **one to ten-year storm events**. *Bioswale* pp. 182-183

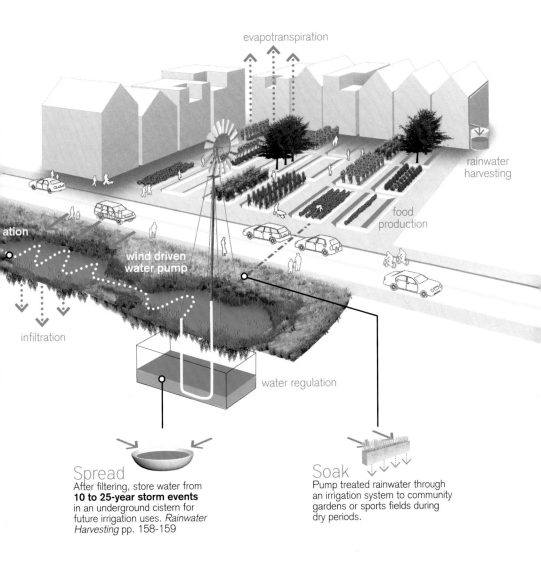

evapotranspiration

rainwater harvesting

food production

ation

wind driven water pump

infiltration

water regulation

Spread
After filtering, store water from **10 to 25-year storm events** in an underground cistern for future irrigation uses. *Rainwater Harvesting* pp. 158-159

Soak
Pump treated rainwater through an irrigation system to community gardens or sports fields during dry periods.

Greenways

open space

Connect open spaces to create an urban greenway that maintains nutrient, natural resource, and habitat flows through the city.

Greenways are an essential connective tissue in open space networks. These pathways preserve and restore nature in urban developments, and have the ability to revitalize underutilized urban sectors. Their delivery of ecological, economic, and social services ensure their favored status as important planning tools. While open space networks will be enjoyed at a local level, regional coordination is often essential for comprehensive design solutions using an ecological approach to development.

Besides creating value for abutting properties and generating economic activity, greenways provide alternative transportation systems free of traffic conflict, and are ideal for casual transit and recreation. They also improve health by accommodating active living and physical activity. Greenways are key to large-scale stormwater treatment and flood protection, acting as vegetated buffers and flood basins that minimize property damage from flooding.

Besides use of the greenway as an agricultural belt or a rails to trails conversion, its most significant incarnation is the riparian buffer. A riparian buffer is part of a larger system known as the riparian corridor, which consists of a floodplain, stream banks, and a stream channel. Riparian buffers are important ecotones between land and water, offering unique habitat while regulating sediment inputs from upland land uses. Riparian buffers are essential to sustaining healthy streams and watersheds.

Slow

Implement flow control devices such as curbs and level spreaders to slow the flow of water before reaching the greenway. *Flow Control Devices* pp. 148-149

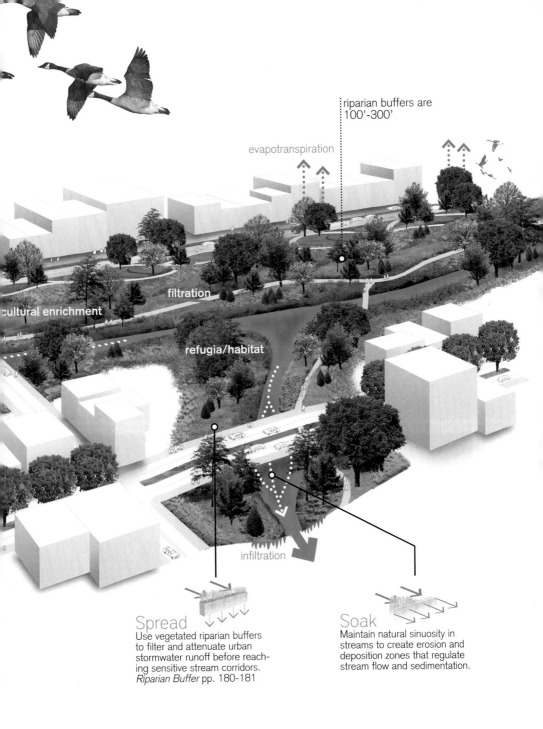

riparian buffers are
100'-300'

evapotranspiration

filtration

cultural enrichment

refugia/habitat

infiltration

Spread
Use vegetated riparian buffers to filter and attenuate urban stormwater runoff before reaching sensitive stream corridors.
Riparian Buffer pp. 180-181

Soak
Maintain natural sinuosity in streams to create erosion and deposition zones that regulate stream flow and sedimentation.

Greenway Crossing Design Principles

Greenway functioning can be compromised if intersections with streets are not properly designed. Streets can be designed to protect natural resources through alignment with topography and natural features. Reduction in the frequency of crossings and design of low-impact crossings are particularly important. Periodically, vehicular crossings may be replaced with pedestrian and bicycle-only bridges. Stream crossing intervals should occur no closer than 600 (high density) to 1,200 (medium density) feet and should be restricted to major roads. Other considerations for greenway crossings include: 1) bridge crossings are to be at a right angle to the channel to minimize shading of the stream; 2) foundation levels of bridges are to be below the deepest point of the stream within the respective reach; 3) bridge soffits are to be a minimum of one foot above the height of adjacent banks, high enough to allow wildlife passage; and 4) bridge structure shall be set back behind the unbroken bank, minimizing impediments to stream flow.

evapotranspiratio

recreation

filtration

bridge structure in stream channel impedes water flow and is prone to frequent flooding

street | pervious sidewalk | filt

evapotranspiration

climate
regulation

refugia/
habitat

erosion control
and sediment
retention

nutrient
cycling

wildlife corridor

filtration

infiltration

:r strip|riparian edge|stream channel|riparian edge|

|f l o o d p l a i n|

What are the LID facilities?

The LID Facilities Menu organizes facilities based on increasing level of treatment service (quality) as well as increasing level of volume reduction (quantity). Therefore, number one (1), flow control devices offer the least amount of treatment services while number twenty-one (21), constructed wetland offers the most. Most municipalities require drainage infrastructure to manage 100-year storm events. Though one facility alone will not likely satisfy performance requirements, facilities with varying levels of service in a treatment network will provide superior levels of treatment and volume reduction.

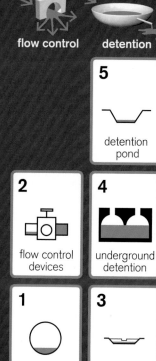

flow control   **detention**

5

detention pond

2

flow control devices

4

underground detention

1

oversized pipes

3

dry swale

from mechanical ———

retention   filtration   infiltration   treatment

8 retention pond

11 surface sand filter

15 infiltration trench

18 riparian buffer

21 constructed wetland

7 rainwater harvesting

10 underground sand filter

13 vegetated roof

14 pervious paving

17 rain garden

20 infiltration basin

6 wet vault

9 filter strip

12 vegetated wall

16 tree box filter

19 bioswale

increasing level of volume reduction →

→ to biological

LID Facilities Menu

LID Facility Selection

Selection of the optimum LID facility or combination of facilities for a project or site depends on the desired hydrologic outcomes. While site planning techniques can greatly reduce the hydrologic impacts of development, additional measures are likely needed to mimic pre-development hydrology—the goal of LID. Once the site hydrology has been analyzed for pre-development conditions and post-development objectives, the site can be shaped through design of a LID treatment network.

The first step in determining LID facility selection requires an evaluation of site opportunities and constraints. Opportunities involve physical conditions of a site, such as soils (infiltration rate), water table depth, bedrock depth, climate, drainage area, precipitation patterns, slope and available land. These physical conditions influence the types of facilities to be used. Therefore, an understanding of the project site is critical to LID facility selection (see "The LID Watershed Approach" pp. 30-43). Remember to think small in regards to the size of the managed area, which encourages a network of smaller, distributed facilities in place of one large facility.

The second step in determining LID facility selection is to define the type of hydrologic controls required. Hydrologic controls include flow control, detention, retention, filtration, infiltration and treatment. Control functions are quantifiable for pre-development conditions based on various design parameters such as stormwater runoff volume, peak discharge, and frequency and duration of discharge. Like conventional stormwater management infrastructure, LID networks must meet local stormwater rate, volume, and water quality treatment mandates for post-development conditions.

Other site feasibility factors include maintenance and management protocols, community acceptance, and cost. Facility selection is not just a matter of choosing from a menu of preferred practices, but rather is part of a larger planning and design process. The facilities by themselves may not be sufficient in restoring the hydrologic functions of a site. LID solutions are most effective when combined with other site planning practices described in "How can we implement LID?" pp. 44-141.

Third, facilities are arranged on site in varying configurations to determine if they meet both site constraints and local regulations, measured by hydrological modeling. Due to multiple variables, facilities are arranged and sized until hydrologic control objectives are optimized. This interactive process usually identifies several design options that meet the development goals. The final configuration can then be determined by space requirements, site aesthetics and cost.

If LID facilities alone cannot meet the hydrologic control objectives of a project it may be necessary to create a hybrid solution, incorporating conventional hard engineering practices. Severe site constraints, such as soils with low infiltration rates, the location of the water table, and intensive land uses, may render LID facilities insufficient. Nonetheless, LID facilities should be used wherever possible, supplemented by conventional practices such as detention ponds and pipes to meet hydrologic design objectives.

Information on LID facility selection from: *Low-Impact Development Design Strategies: An Integrated Design Approach*, prepared by Prince George's County, Maryland

oversized
pipes

Oversized Pipes

Oversized pipes are subsurface pipe systems sized larger than required to reduce peak flow rates.

While oversized pipes are more costly, they eliminate larger pressure drops and high velocities associated with undersized, or even correctly sized pipes during larger storm events. Lower velocities reduce outlet erosion and scouring. Larger volume pipes allow water to be detained, without creating problematic backwater effects. The location of oversized pipes can vary within the LID network.

As with any pipe infrastructure, oversized pipes require trash and sediment removal annually.

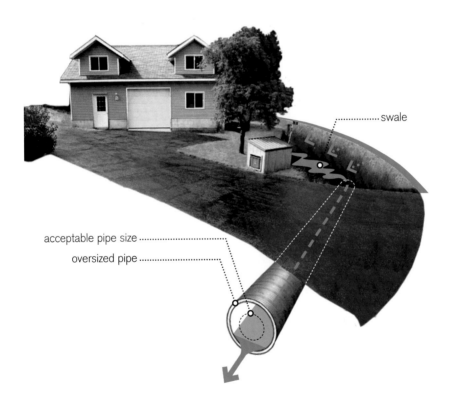

swale

acceptable pipe size

oversized pipe

References:
Minnesota Urban Small Sites BMP Manual

optimal level of service
flow control

location in LID network
downstream from concentrated
stormwater runoff

scale
from small residential application to
larger commercial site

management regime
trash and sediment removal as
needed

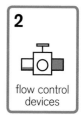

2

flow control
devices

Flow Control Devices

Flow control devices, such as flow splitters, are used to reduce peak discharge, attenuating concentrated stormwater flows.

These devices are placed in areas of concentrated sheet flow, channel flow, or pipe flow to attenuate stormwater runoff prior to it entering a stormwater management system. Flow control devices slow concentrated surface runoff and pipe discharge, thus allowing large debris and sediments to drop out of suspension. These devices are intended to improve the function of other LID facilities and prevent scouring from excessive flow energy. Damaging runoff, peak flow rates, and sediment loads that overwhelm stormwater management systems, are reduced as a result of using flow control devices.

These facilities require regular management and inspection to remove excess sediment, trash, and debris.

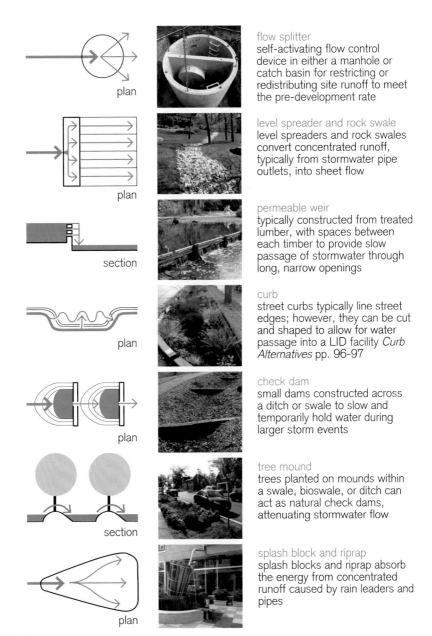

flow splitter
self-activating flow control device in either a manhole or catch basin for restricting or redistributing site runoff to meet the pre-development rate

plan

level spreader and rock swale
level spreaders and rock swales convert concentrated runoff, typically from stormwater pipe outlets, into sheet flow

plan

permeable weir
typically constructed from treated lumber, with spaces between each timber to provide slow passage of stormwater through long, narrow openings

section

curb
street curbs typically line street edges; however, they can be cut and shaped to allow for water passage into a LID facility *Curb Alternatives* pp. 96-97

plan

check dam
small dams constructed across a ditch or swale to slow and temporarily hold water during larger storm events

plan

tree mound
trees planted on mounds within a swale, bioswale, or ditch can act as natural check dams, attenuating stormwater flow

section

splash block and riprap
splash blocks and riprap absorb the energy from concentrated runoff caused by rain leaders and pipes

plan

References:
Low Impact Development Design Strategies–An Integrated Design Approach
Low Impact Development Manual for Michigan

optimal level of service
detention/filtration/infiltration

location in LID network
downstream of flow control facilities,
upstream of catchment components,
overflow basins, or outlets

scale
small watershed runoff area, like low
density projects or small impervious
surfaces

management regime
semiannual inspection for erosion, and
removal of sediment and debris

3

dry swale

Dry Swale

A dry swale, or grassed swale, is an open grassed conveyance channel that filters, attenuates, and detains stormwater runoff as it moves downstream.

In place of hard-engineered concrete channels, dry swales offer services beyond peak flow reduction that include runoff detention and sedimentation. Dry swales, when combined with check dams and underdrains, detain stormwater, and increase infiltration. Often located in drainage easements, they are a cost effective way to convey water between buildings, land uses, and along roadsides. Water quality is optimized when the channel profile is two to eight foot maximum in bottom width, holding a four inch water volume depth. During the establishment newly seeded banks should be stabilized with erosion control devices.

Dry swales can improve site aesthetics and provide wildlife habitat, depending on the type of grasses planted. Periodic inspections of dry swales are needed in order to manage grass growth, and remove large debris and/or trash. Annual inspections should assess the slope of the dry swale, as well as the infiltration rate.

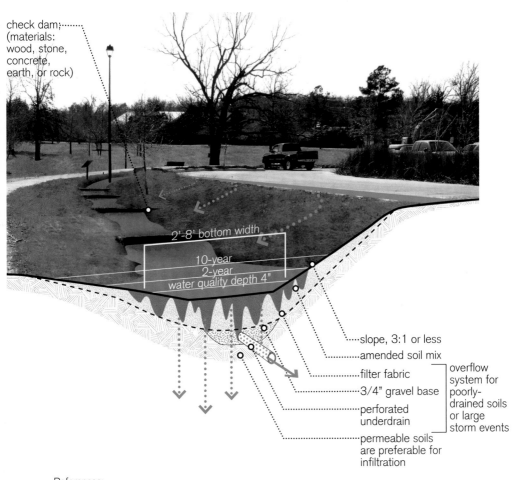

check dam;
(materials:
wood, stone,
concrete,
earth, or rock)

2'-8' bottom width

10-year
2-year
water quality depth 4"

slope, 3:1 or less

amended soil mix

filter fabric

3/4" gravel base

perforated
underdrain

permeable soils
are preferable for
infiltration

overflow
system for
poorly-
drained soils
or large
storm events

References:
Low Impact Development Design Strategies–An Integrated Design Approach
Low Impact Development Manual for Michigan
United States Department of Housing and Urban Development
Stormwater Management Handbook
Minnesota Urban Small Sites BMP Manual

optimal level of service
detention/infiltration

location in LID network
optimally placed after filtration facilities
to prevent excessive sedimentation

scale
maximum watershed runoff area is 25
acres

management regime
inspection and sediment cleanout

4

underground
detention

Underground Detention

Underground detention systems detain stormwater runoff prior to its entrance into a conveyance system.

Underground storage systems store and slowly release runoff into the LID network. Some systems can infiltrate stormwater if the soil beneath is permeable. Underground storage is employed in places where available surface area for on-grade storage is limited.

Underground storage reduces peak flow rate through metered discharge and has potential for infiltration. Improved water quality is achieved by sedimentation, or the settling of suspended solids. Though at first costly, underground detention systems are easy to access and maintain.

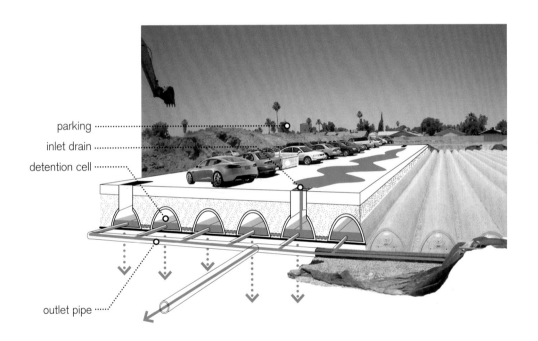

parking

inlet drain

detention cell

outlet pipe

References:
Low Impact Development Manual for Michigan
Urban Design Tools–Low Impact Development
Minnesota Urban Small Sites BMP Manual

optimal level of service
detention

location in LID network
downstream of catchment
and runoff, upstream from off-site
stormwater management systems

scale
watershed runoff area of 10 acres
and greater

management regime
regular trash and intermittent
sediment removal, pollutants
accumulate in soils and may require
amendments and clean out

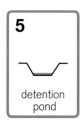

5

detention
pond

Detention Pond

Detention ponds, or dry ponds, are stormwater basins designed to intercept stormwater runoff for temporary impoundment and metered discharge to a conveyance system or a receiving waterbody.

Detention ponds are designed to completely evacuate water from storm events, usually within 24 hours. They primarily provide runoff volume control reducing peak flows that cause downstream scouring and loss of aquatic habitat. As a general rule, detention ponds should be implemented for drainage areas greater than 10 acres. On smaller sites it may be difficult to provide control since outlet diameter specifications needed to control small storm events are small and thus prone to clogging. Also, treatment costs per acre are reduced when implemented at larger scales.

Re-suspension of settled material is a large concern in these systems, requiring periodic sediment, debris, and pollutant removal. Detention ponds do not provide infiltration and are therefore best used within a network that provides biological treatment.

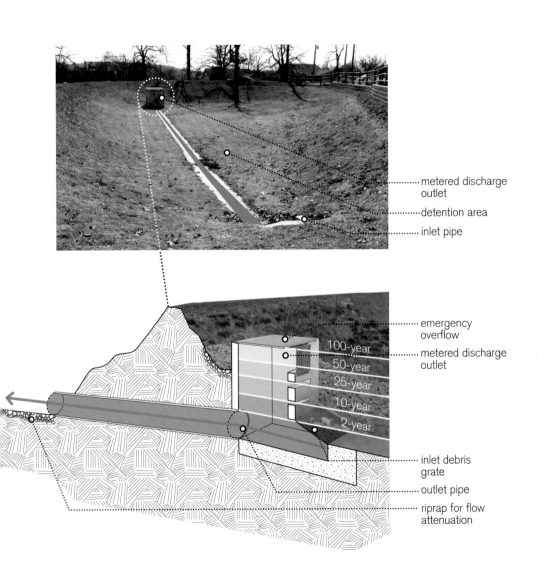

metered discharge outlet

detention area

inlet pipe

emergency overflow

metered discharge outlet

100-year

50-year

25-year

10-year

2-year

inlet debris grate

outlet pipe

riprap for flow attenuation

References:
Low Impact Development Manual for Michigan
Minnesota Urban Small Sites BMP Manual

optimal level of service
retention

location in LID network
upstream of overflow basins or
outlets and downstream from filtration
facilities

scale
sized according to watershed runoff
area

management regime
requires special equipment for trash
and sediment removal

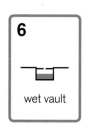

Wet Vault

Wet vaults are subterranean structures for stormwater runoff retention where a permanent pool is maintained.

Wet vaults contribute to stormwater flow attenuation, as well as minor treatment. As a result of permanent water retention, wet vaults are able to remove more sediment than other subterranean storage devices, which drain completely. Wet vaults do not empty in between storm events, but do slowly discharge storage into other stormwater facilities. This facility provides runoff volume control, peak discharge reduction, sediment control, and harvesting potential.

Wet vaults are typically used where there is limited surface area for LID facilities. Minimal maintenance is required. Periodic inspection of in-flow areas is needed along with removal of large debris, sediment, and settled pollutants.

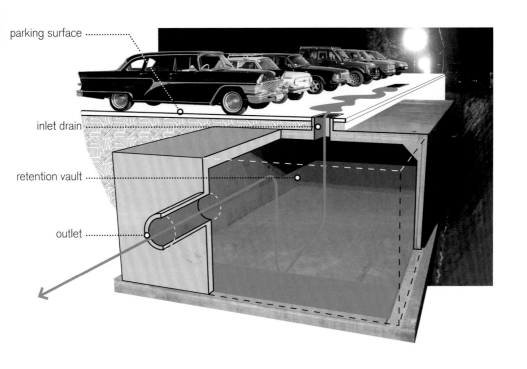

parking surface

inlet drain

retention vault

outlet

References:
Minnesota Urban Small Sites BMP Manual

optimal level of service
retention

location in LID network
beginning of treatment train, directly
at the source of runoff

scale
from a small 50-gallon rain barrel
for a residential application to larger
25,000-gallon commercial scale
cisterns

management regime
seasonal debris removal, storage tank
inspection

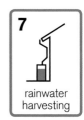

7

rainwater
harvesting

Rainwater Harvesting

Rainwater harvesting involves collection, storage, and reuse of runoff from roofs.

Rainwater harvesting reduces runoff volume and peak flows. Cisterns, bladder tanks, and precast ferrocement septic tanks are generally larger than rain barrels and slim tanks, and are used for domestic water supply, rather than irrigation for landscaping. Most rainwater harvesting devices are modulated and can be connected to provide increased storage. Consider that in areas with rainfall more than 25 inches annually, a 1,000 square foot roof will produce a minimum of 15,000 gallons of rainwater per year. To capture this water for irrigation during the peak months approximately 10 rain barrels or one 500-gallon cistern are needed.

Maintenance needs are moderate compared to other LID technologies, however, water must be used periodically between rain events to maximize storage capacity, minimize runoff, and avoid odors. Gutter screens prevent the accumulation of debris in runoff. Filtration and purification equipment must be incorporated when using stormwater runoff for potable uses.

sealed lid to
keep insects out

inlet

overflow

spigot

concrete pad

rain barrel

typically a 50-gallon barrel that can be utilized at each downspout of a building

slim tank

a slim tank provides smaller storage facilities that can be distributed around the building

plastic, fiberglass, metal, or wood cistern

most common means of rainwater storage and typically used in above grade applications

precast ferrocement septic tank

cement septic tank used instead for rainwater harvesting and can be installed below grade or above the ground

bladder tank

bladders do not require structure and can be placed in any location, thus are an affordable and attractive alternative to other fixed tank systems

References:
Low Impact Development Manual for Michigan
Low Impact Development Technical Guidance Manual for Puget Sound
United States Department of Housing and Urban Development
Minnesota Urban Small Sites BMP Manual
http://www.harvestingrainwater.com

optimal level of service
retention/treatment

location in LID network
downstream of catchment and runoff,
usually constructed at the lowest point
of the site

scale
can be used for residential,
commercial, and industrial sites, with
watershed runoff areas no smaller
than 10 acres depending on regional
precipitation

management regime
inspected semiannually to confirm that
drainage is functioning properly and to
remove sediment, accumulated trash,
and debris

Retention Pond

A retention pond, also known as a wet pool or wet pond, is a constructed stormwater pond that retains a permanent pool of water, with minor biological treatment.

Wet ponds remove pollutants through biological uptake processes and sedimentation. The amount of pollutants that are removed from stormwater runoff is proportionate to the length of time runoff remains in the pond, as well as the relation of runoff to retention pond volume. Since retention ponds must maintain a permanent pool, they cannot be constructed in areas with insufficient precipitation or highly permeable soils, unless the soil is compacted or overlain with clay. Generally, continual drainage inputs are required to maintain permanent pool levels.

One advantage of a retention pond is the presence of aquatic habitat when properly planted and maintained. The use of a pond aerator is necessary to prevent stagnation and algae growth that can lead to eutrophication, or an anaerobic environment. A balanced aerobic environment is a necessary condition for aquatic life and pest control. Regular maintenance inspections are needed to ensure proper drainage, aerobic functioning and aeration, and vegetative health. Trash, debris, and sediment will need to be removed periodically.

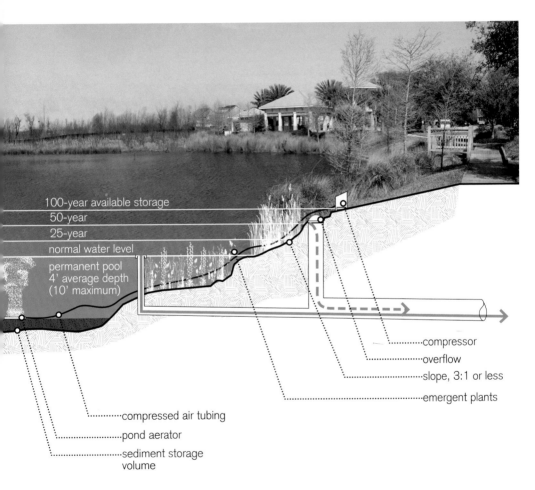

100-year available storage
50-year
25-year
normal water level
permanent pool
4' average depth
(10' maximum)

compressor
overflow
slope, 3:1 or less
emergent plants

compressed air tubing
pond aerator
sediment storage
volume

References:
Low Impact Development Manual for Michigan
Minnesota Urban Small Sites BMP Manual
EPA Storm Water Technology Fact Sheet-Wet Detention Ponds

optimal level of service
filtration

location in LID network
upstream of major treatment systems

scale
from a small slope at streetside to the
size of a large field

management regime
trash and sediment removal, and
mowing

9

filter strip

Filter Strip

A filter strip is a sloped medium that attenuates stormwater runoff by converting it into sheet flow, typically located parallel to an impervious surface such as a parking lot, driveway, or roadway.

Filter strips use vegetation to slow runoff, allowing suspended sediment and debris loads to drop out of runoff flow. This prevents clogging of stormwater drainage systems or receiving waterbodies. Stormwater runoff should be uniformly distributed along the top of the entire filter strip using a flow control facility such as a level spreader. Other treatment facilities, such as a swale, should be used for channelized flows. The drainage area should not exceed 150 linear feet to ensure proper functioning of the filter strip. The lateral slope of the filter strip should be one to two percent. A series of stepped level spreaders could compensate for slightly steeper slopes.

Filter strip areas cannot be used for construction material storage or activities that could disturb the ground surface. Regular inspection and maintenance are required to prevent clogging by sediment and/or debris. Filter strips should be located in sunny areas to dry out between rain events.

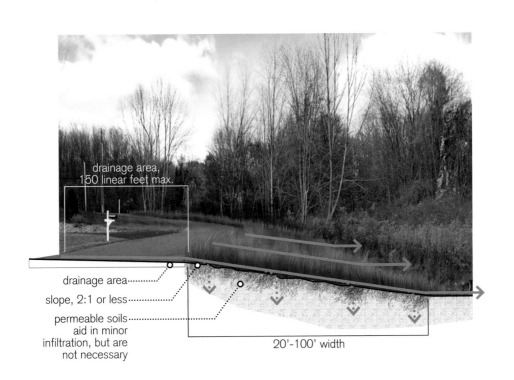

drainage area,
150 linear feet max.

drainage area

slope, 2:1 or less

permeable soils
aid in minor
infiltration, but are
not necessary

20'-100' width

References:
Low Impact Development Design Strategies–An Integrated Design Approach
Low Impact Development Manual for Michigan
United States Department of Housing and Urban Development
Minnesota Urban Small Sites BMP Manual

optimal level of service
detention/filtration

location in LID network
downstream of flow control device
that routes "first flush" of runoff into
the filter

scale
small watershed runoff areas between
one and ten acres

management regime
regular removal of trash, pollutants,
and sediments

10

underground
sand filter

Underground Sand Filter

An underground sand filter is a three chambered system that pretreats, filters, and temporarily stores the first flush of stormwater runoff.

Underground sand filters compensate for space limitations in high-density urban cores lacking pervious drainage areas. Underground sand filters have demonstrated effectiveness in removing many common pollutants found in urban stormwater runoff, especially those in particulate form. Underground sand filters are intended primarily for quality control, not quantity. They are most effective when designed to intercept only the first flush, while subsequent runoff bypasses the system for stormwater quantity control facilities.

These devices are to be used only after a site has been stabilized, as sediment suspended in stormwater runoff during construction would rapidly clog and disable the sand filter.

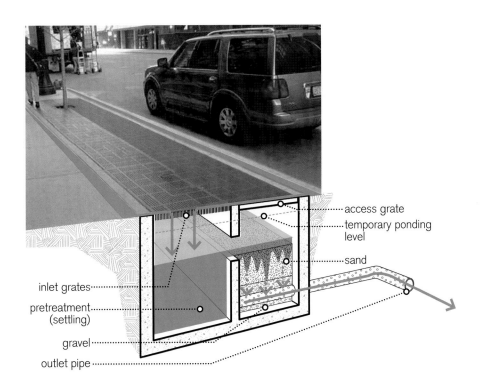

inlet grates

pretreatment
(settling)

gravel

outlet pipe

access grate

temporary ponding
level

sand

References:
Low Impact Development Manual for Michigan
Minnesota Urban Small Sites BMP Manual

optimal level of service
detention/filtration

location in LID network
downstream of flow control device
that routes "first flush" of runoff into
the filter

scale
small watershed runoff areas between
one and ten acres

management regime
regular removal of trash, pollutants,
and sediments

11

surface sand
filter

Surface Sand Filter

Also known as a filtration basin, a surface sand filter utilizes a flow splitter, wet/dry sedimentation forebay, and sand filter bed to manage nutrient loads in the first flush of runoff.

Sand filters receive the first flush of runoff, settling out heavier solids in the pretreatment basin. Water is distributed over the sand filter for a second filtration of pollutants. Surface sand filters trap nitrates, phosphates, hydrocarbons, metals, and sediment. They also reduce peak discharge by collecting and slowing runoff velocity as water flows through the filter.

Surface sand filters are useful for areas where pollutants are a critical water quality issue. Treatment levels provided by these facilities increase when groundwater infiltration is part of the system. Surface sand filters are most efficient when draining less than 10 acres of land.

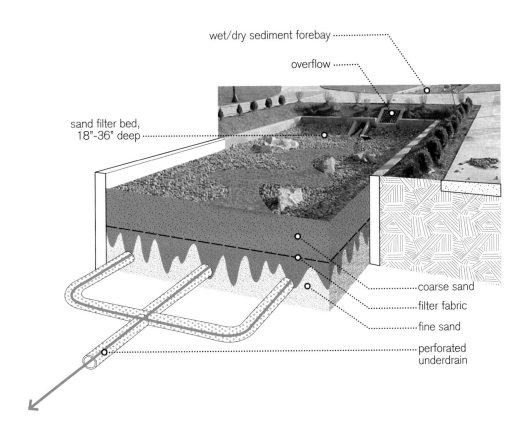

wet/dry sediment forebay

overflow

sand filter bed,
18"-36" deep

coarse sand

filter fabric

fine sand

perforated
underdrain

References:
Low Impact Development Manual for Michigan
Minnesota Urban Small Sites BMP Manual

optimal level of service
flow control/filtration

location in LID network
beginning of network, directly from
the roof

scale
from small residential applications to
larger commercial applications

management regime
occasional watering and trimming
depending on species

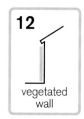

12

vegetated
wall

Vegetated Wall

A vegetated wall, also known as a living or green wall or vertical garden, is an extension of the building envelope laminated with vegetation and a soil or inorganic growing medium.

Vegetated walls are classified as passive or active systems. While active systems address air quality, passive systems address water quality, and thus are more applicable to LID. Similar in application to vegetated roofs, vegetated walls harvest water to reduce stormwater runoff loads. Vegetated walls also regulate building temperature through additional thermal insulation, reducing heating and cooling loads.

Structural loads and proper moisture barriers must be carefully considered, as well as plant types suitable for the intended solar orientation.

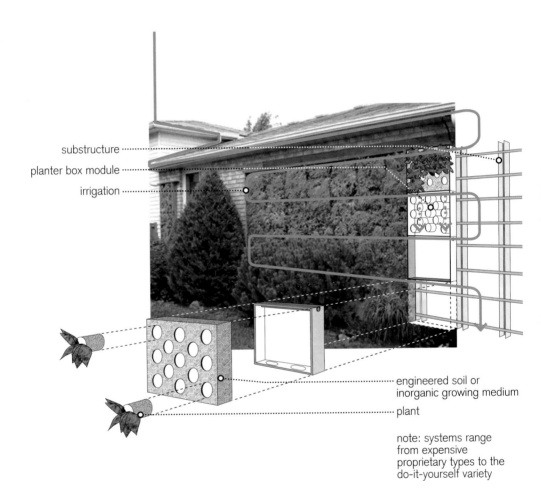

substructure ....

planter box module ....

irrigation ....

engineered soil or
inorganic growing medium

plant

note: systems range
from expensive
proprietary types to the
do-it-yourself variety

References:
Green Roofs for Healthy Cities: Introduction to Green Walls
http://folderofideas.blogspot.com/2009/02/vertical-garden-by-joost-bakker.html
http://www.verticalgardenpatrickblanc.com

169

optimal level of service
filtration/treatment

location in LID network
beginning of network, directly within
the runoff source

scale
from small residential applications to
large industrial buildings

management regime
inspection of the roof membrane, as
well as routine vegetation inspection
and maintenance of the drainage flow
paths

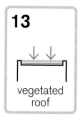

13

vegetated
roof

Vegetated Roof

Vegetated roofs, or green roofs, are garden ecologies installed atop buildings.

Intended to be closed loop systems, vegetated roofs collect rainwater at its source, slow its release, and reduce its volume through evapotranspiration from plants. Vegetated roofs also regulate building temperature through additional thermal insulation, reducing heating and cooling loads. Vegetated roofs are especially effective in controlling intense, short-duration storms, and have been shown to reduce cumulative annual runoff by 50 percent in temperate climates. Vegetated roofs are desirable in flood-prone climates with regular flash storm events.

Vegetated roofs can be built on flat roofs or sloped roofs, however flat roofs are easier to install. Roofs with steep slopes usually require the addition of cross-battens to secure drainage layers and to control soil erosion.

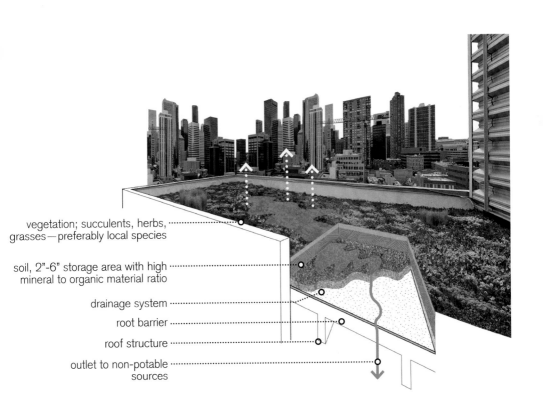

vegetation; succulents, herbs, grasses—preferably local species

soil, 2"-6" storage area with high mineral to organic material ratio

drainage system

root barrier

roof structure

outlet to non-potable sources

References:
Low Impact Development Design Strategies–An Integrated Design Approach
Low Impact Development Manual for Michigan
Low Impact Development Guidance Manual for Puget Sound
Stormwater Management Handbook
Minnesota Urban Small Sites BMP Manual

optimal level of service
filtration/infiltration/treatment

location in LID network
apply upstream of treatment systems
to provide sediment removal and to
reduce runoff volume

scale
from a parking stall to a parking lot or
street

management regime
vacuum-based sediment removal
from paving; turf paver systems may
need to be mowed and irrigated to
maintain vegetation

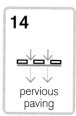

14

pervious
paving

Pervious Paving

Pervious, or permeable, paving allows water to vertically flow through hard surfaces. As substitutes for impervious paving, they support both pedestrian and vehicular traffic.

A pervious paving system includes a subsurface base made of course aggregate for stormwater storage. In some designs, pervious pavement is supported by underground layers of soil, gravel and sand to increase storage and maximize infiltration rates. Pervious paving removes sediment and other pollutants. It acts to reduce and distribute stormwater volume, encouraging groundwater infiltration. Multiple types of pervious paving, including modulated precast pavers, poured in place systems, porous asphalt, porous concrete, and gravel, offer varying levels of service. Reduction of the urban heat island effect is possible when using high-albedo, lightly colored systems.

Large scale vacuums must be used to clean out gravel, paver, and porous systems. Turf paver systems may need occasional mowing and irrigation (see "Surface Materials" pp. 78-79).

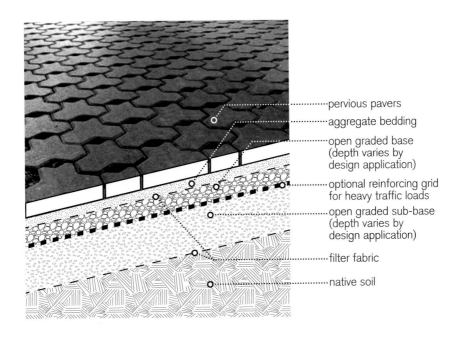

pervious pavers

aggregate bedding

open graded base
(depth varies by
design application)

optional reinforcing grid
for heavy traffic loads

open graded sub-base
(depth varies by
design application)

filter fabric

native soil

pervious surface materials

porous asphalt /concrete   open grid pavers   gravel paving   grass concrete paving   turf pavers

References:
Low Impact Development Manual for Michigan
Stormwater Management Handbook
Minnesota Urban Small Sites BMP Manual
Low Impact Development Technical Guidance Manual for Puget Sound

optimal level of service
infiltration/treatment

location in LID network
downstream of filtration components,
but upstream of major treatment
facilities

scale
from a small strip to a sand field with
a maximum catchment area of two
acres

management regime
annual removal of trash and raking to
maintain permeability

15

infiltration
trench

Infiltration Trench

Infiltration trenches are laminated systems with fabric-lined excavations atop a fabric-lined reservoir to increase infiltration.

Infiltration trenches are particularly useful for sites with poorly-drained soils. Runoff gradually percolates through an engineered trench with amended soil over a period of days. Infiltration trenches filter particulates as stormwater runoff moves through the media. These facilities promote algae growth that serves as pollutant digesters. Since the maximum catchment area for infiltration trenches is two acres, it may be necessary to incorporate supporting LID facilities into the stormwater management plan.

Infiltration trenches require less maintenance if upstream pre-treatment facilities like filter strips are used. Trees should not be planted near infiltration trenches. These two actions reduce the potential for clogging the trench. Annual inspection is recommended to remove large debris and/or trash.

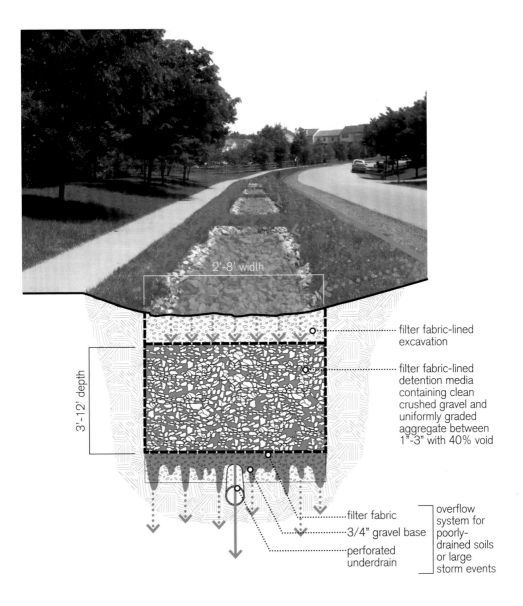

2'-8' width

3'-12' depth

filter fabric-lined excavation

filter fabric-lined detention media containing clean crushed gravel and uniformly graded aggregate between 1"-3" with 40% void

filter fabric

3/4" gravel base

perforated underdrain

overflow system for poorly-drained soils or large storm events

References:
Low Impact Development Design Strategies–An Integrated Design Approach
Low Impact Development Manual for Michigan
United States Department of Housing and Urban Development
Minnesota Urban Small Sites BMP Manual

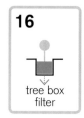

16

tree box
filter

Tree Box Filter

A tree box filter or in ground well consists of a container filled with amended soil and planted with a tree, underlain by crushed gravel media.

Tree root systems treat and uptake stormwater runoff captured from the street into the box filter. An underdrain carries treated runoff to either a surface discharge location or a larger retention system for secondary treatment. The life of the tree is short, so trees need replacement every five to ten years. Tree box filters can also be planted with hardy shrubs and herbaceous plants tolerant of inundations.

Tree box filters and wells can be incorporated into urban retrofits with the added benefits of water quality improvement and reduction of the urban heat island effect. As with other filtration devices, tree box filters require occasional inspection to remove large debris and/or trash.

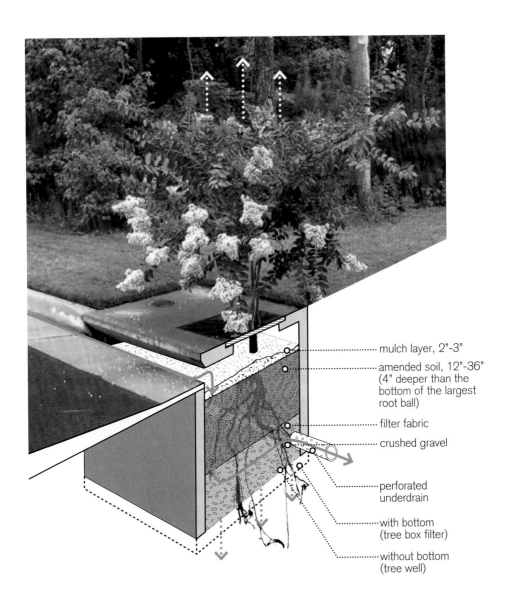

mulch layer, 2"-3"

amended soil, 12"-36"
(4" deeper than the
bottom of the largest
root ball)

filter fabric

crushed gravel

perforated
underdrain

with bottom
(tree box filter)

without bottom
(tree well)

References:
Low Impact Development Manual for Michigan
Urban Design Tools-Low Impact Development
Minnesota Urban Small Sites BMP Manual

optimal level of service
filtration/infiltration/treatment

location in LID network
downstream of filtration facilities,
but upstream of primary treatment
facilities

scale
500 sq ft, to allow for adequate
irrigation between small storm events

management regime
occasional removal of trash and
pruning of vegetation

17

rain
garden

Rain Garden

A rain garden is a planted depression designed to infiltrate stormwater runoff, but not hold it.

A rain garden is commonly known as a bioretention facility. Stormwater pollutant mitigation is accomplished through phytoremediation processes as runoff passes through the plant and soil community. Rain gardens combine layers of organic sandy soil for infiltration, and mulch to promote microbial activity. Native plants are recommended based upon their intrinsic synergies with local climate, soil, and moisture conditions without the use of fertilizers and chemicals. Rain gardens are best applied on a relatively small scale. They work well along driveways and in low lying areas of a property.

Rain gardens should be located at least 10 feet away from buildings to prevent water seepage into foundations or underneath houses, causing mold and mildew problems. Also, location away from large trees allows exposure to sunlight so that rain gardens may dry out between storm events.

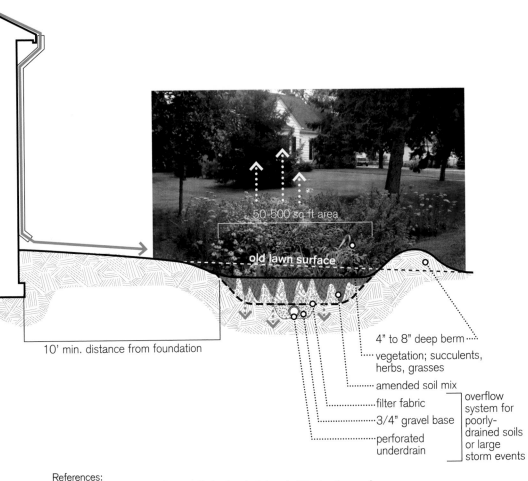

50-500 sq ft area

old lawn surface

10' min. distance from foundation

4" to 8" deep berm ⋯

⋯ vegetation; succulents, herbs, grasses

⋯ amended soil mix

⋯filter fabric

⋯3/4" gravel base

⋯perforated underdrain

overflow system for poorly-drained soils or large storm events

References:
Low Impact Development Design Strategies–An Integrated Design Approach
Low Impact Development Manual for Michigan
Low Impact Development Technical Guidance Manual for Puget Sound
United States Department of Housing and Urban Development
Minnesota Urban Small Sites BMP Manual

optimal level of service
filtration/infiltration/treatment

location in LID network
downstream of all LID facilities, before
waterbodies

scale
100' to 300' wide

management regime
trash and sediment removal as
necessary, and occasional mowing in
zone 3

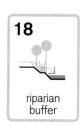

18

riparian
buffer

Riparian Buffer

A riparian buffer is a strip of hydric soil with facultative vegetation along the banks of a river or stream offering niche ecotone services.

Riparian buffers are a simple, inexpensive way to protect and improve water quality through local plant communities. Between 50 and 85 percent of stormwater pollutant loads can be filtered within 100 to 300 foot vegetated buffers. Buffer strips structurally stabilize banks and shorelines to prevent erosion and slumping. Trees and shrubs provide shade to maintain consistent water temperature necessary for nutrient exchange and the survival of some aquatic life. Buffer width is based on surrounding context, soil type, size and slope of catchment area, and vegetative cover.

Riparian buffers are most effective when combined with flow attenuation devices to avoid scouring from high velocity flows throughout a stream channel. Some management is required when riparian buffers are near urban development. Avoid disturbing zone 1 as tree litter aids in flow control and filtration.

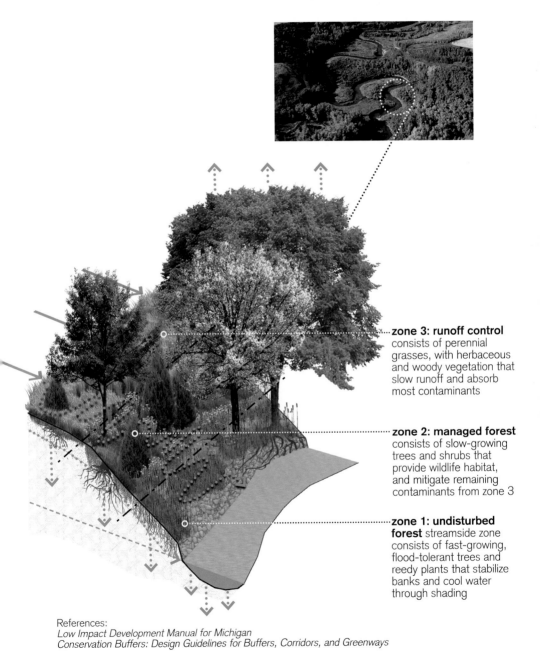

zone 3: runoff control consists of perennial grasses, with herbaceous and woody vegetation that slow runoff and absorb most contaminants

zone 2: managed forest consists of slow-growing trees and shrubs that provide wildlife habitat, and mitigate remaining contaminants from zone 3

zone 1: undisturbed forest streamside zone consists of fast-growing, flood-tolerant trees and reedy plants that stabilize banks and cool water through shading

References:
Low Impact Development Manual for Michigan
Conservation Buffers: Design Guidelines for Buffers, Corridors, and Greenways

optimal level of service
filtration/infiltration/treatment

location in LID network
downstream of filtration components,
but upstream of larger detention,
retention, or treatment facilities

scale
2'-8' wide with 2"-4" optimal water
depth

management regime
occasional removal of trash and
pruning of vegetation

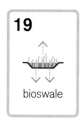

19

bioswale

Bioswale

A bioswale is an open, gently sloped, vegetated channel designed for treatment and conveyance of stormwater runoff.

Bioswales are a bioretention device in which pollutant mitigation occurs through phytoremediation by facultative vegetation. Bioswales combine treatment and conveyance services, reducing land development costs by eliminating the need for costly conventional conveyance systems. The main function of a bioswale is to treat stormwater runoff as it is conveyed, whereas the main function of a rain garden is to treat stormwater runoff as it is infiltrated. Bioswales are usually located along roads, drives, or parking lots where the contributing acreage is less than five acres.

Bioswales require curb cuts, gutters or other devices that direct flow to them. They may require an underdrain where soil permeability is limited, as well as an overflow grate for larger storm events.

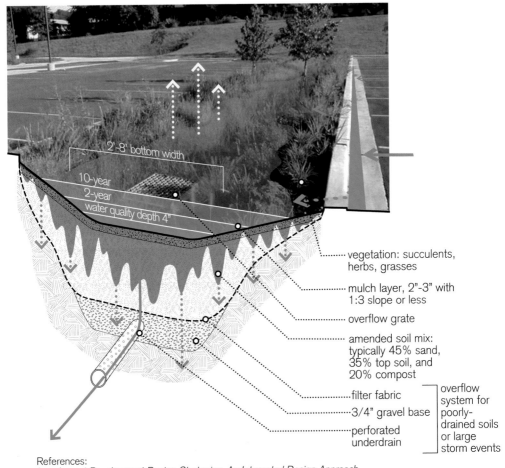

2'-8' bottom width

10-year
2-year
water quality depth 4"

vegetation: succulents, herbs, grasses

mulch layer, 2"-3" with 1:3 slope or less

overflow grate

amended soil mix: typically 45% sand, 35% top soil, and 20% compost

filter fabric

3/4" gravel base

perforated underdrain

overflow system for poorly-drained soils or large storm events

References:
Low Impact Development Design Strategies–An Integrated Design Approach
Low Impact Development Manual for Michigan
Low Impact Development Technical Guidance Manual for Puget Sound
United States Department of Housing and Urban Development
Minnesota Urban Small Sites BMP Manual

optimal level of service
filtration/infiltration/treatment

location in LID network
end-of-line facility, upstream
of overflow basins or receiving
waterbodies

scale
large multi-acre wet meadows

management regime
semiannual removal of trash and
sediment, and mowing

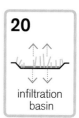

20

infiltration
basin

Infiltration Basin

Infiltration basins, or wet meadows, are shallow impound areas with highly permeable soils designed to temporarily detain and infiltrate stormwater runoff. They do not retain a permanent pool of water.

These facilities improve water quality by filtering stormwater runoff through hydric soils and recharging groundwater supply. In addition to water filtration, infiltration basins use facultative plants for phytoremediation to mitigate pollutants from stormwater runoff. Unlike rain gardens and bioswales, which are primarily used for single property applications, infiltration basins optimally serve larger scales of land development. The key element in siting infiltration basins is identifying areas with intrinsic hydrogeologic properties (minimum soil infiltration rate of 0.27 inches/hour) critical for sustained infiltration. They are not suitable on fill sites.

Since the primary cause of failure in infiltration basins is sediment buildup, sediment-reducing facilities must be used upstream. Infiltration basins require less maintenance as vegetation communities mature through successive stages of ecological development.

flat basin floor
with dense plant
community

permeable soils with
infiltration rates
> 0.27 inches/hour

deeply-rooted
facultative
vegetation

water table

groundwater

References:
Low Impact Development Manual for Michigan
Minnesota Urban Small Sites BMP Manual

optimal level of service
retention/filtration/infiltration/treatment

location in LID network
end-of-line facility, upstream
of overflow basins or receiving
waterbodies

scale
from pocket wetlands managing up
to 10 acres of drainage to shallow
marshes managing more than 25
acres of drainage

management regime
system requires removal of trash and
sediment between two and ten years,
and semiannually during first three
years

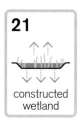

21

constructed
wetland

Constructed Wetland

Constructed wetlands are artificial marshes or swamps with permanent standing water that offer a full range of ecosystem services to treat polluted stormwater.

Considered to be a comprehensive treatment system, constructed wetlands, like infiltration basins, require intrinsic hydrogeologic properties to reproduce natural watershed functioning. As with other infiltration systems, pre-treatment systems upstream help to remove sediment that may clog a wetland system, resulting in eutrophication or an oxygen deprived system.

Constructed wetlands are land rich biofilters and differ from retention ponds in their shallower depths, greater vegetation coverage, and extensive wildlife habitat. They require relatively large contributing drainage areas to maintain a shallow permanent pool. Minimum contributing drainage area should be at least 10 acres, although pocket wetlands may be appropriate for smaller sites if sufficient water flow is available.

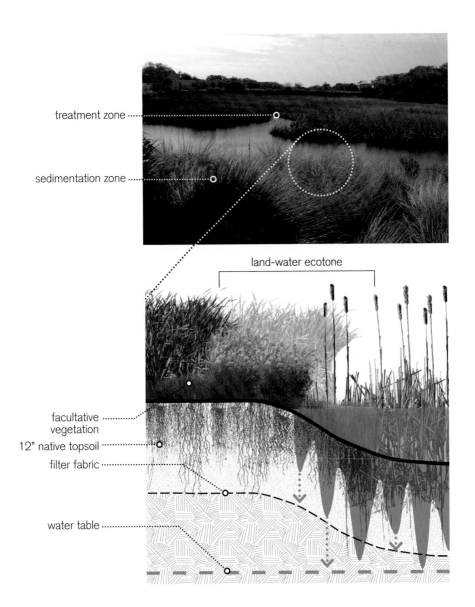

treatment zone

sedimentation zone

land-water ecotone

facultative vegetation

12" native topsoil

filter fabric

water table

References:
Low Impact Development Manual for Michigan
United States Department of Housing and Urban Development
Minnesota Urban Small Sites BMP Manual

What can you do?

Decision making incorporates diverse stakeholder interests, emphasizing shared efforts among public and private realms that account for local, state, and national objectives. Stakeholder agency at the levels of property owners, design and construction professionals, and municipalities hold the greatest promise for implementing comprehensive LID practices in urban land management. This section clarifies how LID can be integrated into our current systems of development for a true watershed approach and explains the collateral economic and social benefits.

what role you play
pp. 190-195

**policies, codes,
and covenants**
pp. 196-205

**management, not
maintenance**
pp. 206-211

Property Owners

Property owners, from small-lot single-family homeowners to large commercial developers, constitute the largest demand market for stormwater management, and consequently wield significant influence toward realizing a LID watershed approach. The cumulative impact of owner land management in eliminating nonpoint source pollution is tremendous.

Indeed, just as pollution in headwaters and small streams has a greater impact on watershed health than pollution in larger waterbodies, development impacts from individual property parcels have an equally compounding effect on watershed quality.

Property owners should understand that in LID their properties become part of a larger landscape infrastructure serving the public interest, and are no longer just decorative landscapes.

Recommended LID implementation steps for property owners include development of facultative landscapes using native plants recommended by local nurseries and gardening experts. Other steps involve minimization of impervious surfaces, and harvesting and/or filtration of stormwater runoff from buildings. Owners involved in subdivision and campus projects should hire design and construction professionals offering LID expertise.

Collateral Benefits to Property Owners

- Increase in property values due to the presence of well-designed and functional landscapes that facilitate best stormwater management practices.

- Time devoted to yard maintenance is reduced since LID landscapes achieve greater self-organization as they age, nullifying the need for continual mowing, trimming, and blowing beyond occasional pruning.

- Maintenance and energy costs are reduced since plant biodiversity in LID landscapes negates the need for fertilizers, herbicides, and mowing—all based on non-renewable fossil fuel inputs. Use of native xeriscapes obviates the need for continual irrigation beyond the establishment phase, lowering water bills.

- Higher aesthetic value (not to mention economic value) is derived from the changing floristic structure in native polycultural landscapes than that from the monoculture of the industrialized turf lawn.

Design and Construction Professionals

The professional design community, including planners, ecologists, architects, engineers, landscape architects, contractors, and developers that possess a comprehensive knowledge of LID represent the most influential sector for mainstreaming LID practices. This requires professionals and their organizations to undertake advocacy and education efforts with clients, the public, and policymakers.

Design industry professionals, typically focused on the sustainability and performance of their individual products—whether a building, landscape, or subdivision—should understand the lifecycle impacts of their project design within the context of its watershed.

Construction industry professionals should understand the proper site staging techniques that facilitate LID functioning after construction.

Recommended LID implementation steps for building professionals include design and construction with consideration for the watershed within which the property is located as the minimum planning unit. Professionals need to adopt greater interdisciplinary collaborations and work processes related to site analysis and design. Design for hydrology first, then follow with project component design and construction staging.

Collateral Benefits to Design and Construction Professionals

- Expand environmental expertise and subsequent range of professional services offered to the public. Since stronger water protection laws are being legislated nationwide, such professional services will be needed to meet future market demand.

- Create market demand for good design and planning, supported by enabling policy-making. Some public sector clients are already requesting LID services.

- Place professional design and planning communities in new leadership and education roles concerning the built environment, which enhances the professions' standings with the public.

- Increase the range of ecological services in completed work products, constituting premium design and construction results with comparable or lower budgets.

Municipalities

As code-setting bodies that establish and enforce public policy, municipalities together with water utility authorities, hold the single greatest influence in determining a community's development patterns. Indeed, if a community has experienced extensive sprawl it is because its codes and land-use regulations have facilitated such sprawl.

Municipalities set development standards and market expectations through codes, incentives, and enforcement. Many municipalities disallow or discourage LID infrastructure at the level of the block, street, and open space, unwittingly compounding water quality problems in their watersheds.

While most municipalities are still fully committed to pipe-and-pond infrastructure, a few have substituted parks for pipes. The potential shortcoming of LID is that it remains a lot-specific management strategy in land-rich suburban contexts, never having risen to the level of infrastructure in dense, urban contexts.

Recommended implementation steps for municipalities include development of LID ordinances rather than reliance on variances. Municipalities can also incentivize LID adoption, signaling to the finance and development communities their preference for LID as a development template. Water utilities will need to overcome their own specialization and instead function as integrated resource planners that assist municipalities and regions in managing water as a natural resource.

Collateral Benefits to Municipalities

- Improved regional water quality and ecological functioning in watersheds. This is a prerequisite for addressing those waterbodies on the USEPA's 303(d) impaired waters list and seeking their removal from impairment status as per the Clean Water Act of 1972.

- Street costs can be lowered by 40 percent in urban areas of moderate densities since LID applications will not require total hard infrastructure solutions, involving pipes, catchment basins, and curbs and gutters.

- Since vegetated open space becomes the infrastructure in LID, municipalities will enjoy improved ratios of urban park area per resident through water infrastructure investments.

- Decreases in treatment loads and operating costs for those municipalities using wastewater treatment facilities to treat stormwater runoff.

- Improved street aesthetic and safety through development of green streets and resultant mitigation of the urban heat island effect.

Policies, Codes and Covenants

Obstacles to LID

LID is a nonconforming development model in most cities, making it illegal as the primary stormwater management system. Yet everyone familiar with LID—from those who finance projects, to property owners, builders, designers, and city administrators who regulate and approve our built environment—agree that LID is superior to the conventional development model. However, reform is difficult because everyone's models and business plans were formulated around the prevailing hard-engineered model, which ignores watershed functioning and the general concept of ecosystem services. This model creates cognitive barriers for LID implementation, including a lack of local precedent, a perception of risk, and a steep learning curve for the construction industry. Nonetheless, LID infrastructure has been adopted as a by-right development by municipalities that expect more ecological services from their public works investments. The following list highlights commonplace ordinances that function as obstacles to LID implementation. The list also notes regulatory opportunities conducive to LID implementation absent in many ordinances and covenants. Ideally, simple modifications to local codes will encourage builders and property owners to integrate LID technologies, while amplifying public safety.

building

Prohibition of Greywater Recycling for Household Use
Greywater is domestic wastewater generated from dishwashing, laundry, and bathing. Greywater does not include blackwater from toilets, which contains higher amounts of chemical and biological contaminants. Some

municipalities allow greywater recycling for domestic and commercial landscape irrigation, while a few permit recycling for household uses if accompanied by additional treatment systems. The latter is presently costlier than municipal supply, though this may change with the rising energy costs associated with transporting water.

Prohibition of Rainwater Recycling for Household Use

Codes and ordinances nationwide are inconsistent on rainwater harvesting, as some jurisdictions require harvesting systems for new construction while others allow reuse of rainwater for outdoor irrigation only, prohibiting reuse inside. Still others disallow tanks and collection facilities for harvesting altogether, claiming they are eyesores. Some states outline extensive specifications for rainwater harvesting systems, including disinfection requirements for private water systems. Other places allow dual-supply systems, combining harvested water with water from a public utility, accounting for proper backflow prevention so that harvested water does not contaminate the public water source.

Requirement for Gutters

Due to chronic flooding and general site planning failures, some subdivisions require the use of gutters with rain leaders connected to streets for the evacuation of rainwater. This eliminates the consideration of rain gardens and other LID strategies for roof-based runoff.

Sprawling Building Footprints

Building height is regulated by city zoning codes, often at very low densities. One way to reduce runoff is to incentivize more compact building footprints where appropriate. This reduces impervious surfaces by minimizing the overall land area occupied by buildings.

property

Lack of Requirements Regulating Soil Compaction

Since proper functioning of LID facilities depends upon soil percolation rates, special measures must be taken to avoid soil compaction during the construction process and ensure

197

productive and healthy soils after construction. Implement "no compaction zones" in sensitive areas and where LID facilities will be located. Limit construction traffic to staged construction zones where soil compaction will not be an issue. These areas should be identified on construction documents and marked in the field. Require contractors to restore pre-construction soil permeability that has been compacted by construction vehicles. Permeability can be enhanced by rototilling open spaces prior to seeding or planting.

Lack of Requirements for Maintaining Pre-Development Hydrologic Regimes
Stormwater management should be designed to reduce peak flow rates to pre-development levels on a site, the core objective of LID. When assessing pre-development data for an individual property, hydrological modeling at the scale of the larger drainage area is needed for accurate site analysis.

Turf Specifications

The lawn can be a highly litigious area of real estate development. There are numerous municipalities and property owner associations regulations governing lawns, few with ecological performance in mind. Some regulations specify a maximum turf height as short as four inches; others exclusively require non-native short blade grass with a minimum color of green (i.e., dead grass is not allowed). The latter requirement demands extensive irrigation and use of chemical-laden fertilizers, along with herbicides when varietal species (weeds) are prohibited. Many cosmetically-oriented regulations outlaw the use of diverse and rustic plant communities central to xeriscape lawns. Often these LID appropriate lawns are classified as nuisances and subject to fines. Municipalities can encourage alternative turf, such as buffalograss and mixed-seed native grasses, which give the consistent appearance desired without the intensive maintenance regimen.

Excessive Setback Distances in Residential Districts
Most codes have considerable property setback distances for buildings. This reduces building location flexibility, limiting opportunities to preserve sensitive ecological areas

with permeable soils, and potential LID facility locations. In addition, larger setbacks mean longer driveways, which increase total impervious surface areas. Consider that "build-to-street" or "zero-lot" lines can reduce impervious surface areas while offering a shared and cohesive streetscape.

Lack of Requirements for Protecting LID Facilities

Removal of installed LID facilities and infrastructure, including plant systems, should require a permit by municipalities. Trees are also part of the stormwater management infrastructure and should be considered similarly. Removing any part of the stormwater management infrastructure can cause failures.

Prohibition of Permeable Surfaces for Parking

Many municipalities and property owner associations require hard surfaces for on-site parking, eliminating the use of permeable pavers, decorative gravel, Hollywood Driveways (two paved wheel tracks each between 2.5 and 3.5 feet wide, separated by a planted strip at least three feet wide.), or a turf and field stone court. The regulation is not without merit, as dirt driveways generate four times the sediment load of paved surfaces. However, lower density development might consider limits on lot coverage with impervious surfaces (i.e., 15 percent). Also, parking stalls and overflow parking areas can use permeable paving to reduce impervious surface areas, as well as increase treatment capacity.

Excessive Automobile Parking Requirements

Most municipal land-use codes require excessive parking requirements, particularly in large format retail, which has a parking footprint 1.5 times larger than the retail floor area it serves. Also, office buildings require one parking stall for every 100 square feet of office space, which is 300 percent larger when you consider that each parking stall is roughly 300 square feet. Commercial parking lots are sized for peak-load holiday shopping and thus highly underutilized. Lot sizes can be reduced through lot sharing between land uses with different usage patterns without compromising capacity.

Lack of Requirements to Keep Stormwater Runoff On-site
While more states and municipalities are tightening stormwater runoff requirements, many still do not regulate discharges from individual properties. Downstream properties experience damage, especially during periods of peak discharge where neighboring developments have modified site contouring.

Lack of Tree Protection Requirements
Most municipalities do not require preservation or mitigation of existing trees. Municipalities should implement codes that favor the preservation of "heritage trees" larger than eight inches in caliper. However, removal of trees for development may be necessary. In that case, municipalities should develop tree mitigation codes that require replacement of heritage tree types within the development.

Lack of Proper Wetland Mitigation
No wetland of ecological importance should be removed for site development. Many municipalities lack a wetland protection policy or classification system. However, if wetland removal is allowed, an environmental assessment detailing quality and ecological connectivity with a mitigation plan should be prepared. A good mitigation plan will require replacement of the wetland with one at least one and one-half times the size of the wetland removed and of the same quality.

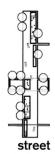

street

Sidewalk Material Restrictions
In the interest of streamlining maintenance and satisfying Americans with Disabilities Act (ADA) standards, some municipalities allow only concrete sidewalk construction.

This excludes consideration of a permeable and recyclable material like rubber, which is adaptive to unstable ground conditions. Concrete sidewalks tend to crack and heave over time, creating impassable and unsafe pedestrian environments.

Universal Requirements for Sidewalks
Currently, many municipalities require sidewalks to be located on both sides of the street in new developments. In order to reduce impervious surface area, allow low density residential neighborhoods to locate a sidewalk on only one side of the street. Also, allow for alternative pedestrian facilities in parks and greenways parallel to the street right-of-way.

Prohibition Of Vegetation Near an Intersection
Currently municipalities prohibit vegetation that grows above three feet in height within 25 feet of an intersection. While this is meant to secure traffic lines-of-sight, it limits the location of LID facilities. Municipalities are now combining LID facilities with traffic calming devices at intersections, like chicanes and bulbouts in street design.

Prohibition of LID Facilities in the Public Right-of-Way
Many municipalities prohibit the use of LID facilities in the public right-of-way due to maintenance concerns, though they will allow the use of LID facilities on private property to meet stormwater management requirements for streets. Shifting public management concerns to the private realm undermines the shared responsibilities defining the watershed approach.

Prohibition of Pervious Materials in Public Right-of-Way
Similar to regulations governing driveways, some municipalities prohibit the use of pervious paving, such as porous concrete or asphalt, due to maintenance concerns. Most municipalities have not yet acquired the street vacuums and other equipment needed to maintain the filtration function of pervious materials; nor have municipalities developed the management protocols for LID streets, as they are still undergoing pilot-level testing.

Prohibition of Runoff Conveyance in Public Right-of-Way
Most municipal street engineering codes prohibit runoff conveyance across a public right-of-way (except for alleys) beyond the loading generated by the street itself. Streets are typically crowned at the center, preventing alternative uses of the street as a sheet flow conduit in a larger LID network.

Minimum Street Widths
Many municipalities, primarily influenced by fire department requirements for emergency access, stipulate construction of wide streets. Contemporary residential neighborhoods will often have 36-foot wide street sections, when 18 to 20 feet would suffice. This has yielded such a dramatic increase in untreated sediment and stormwater runoff loading that some municipalities have established "skinny street" programs to improve water quality, walkability, and traffic safety.

Requirements for Low-Density Land Uses
Low-density development in subdivisions that require one to two units per acre create excessive road lengths in proportion to the number of buildings served. Consider incentivizing compact development that clusters the same amount of units in a smaller footprint, reducing road lengths and impervious surface areas.

Requirement for Street Curbs
Citing ADA, some municipalities require curbs to differentiate between pedestrian and vehicular traffic paths. While other means are available to establish the necessary distinction, this requirement eliminates shared streets and other viable right-of-way configurations that employ flush surfaces for runoff conveyance and treatment.

Arterial Highway Statutes Prohibiting Landscape Materials
As per statutes governing state highway development as outlined in the American Association of State Highway and Transportation Officials—ironically called the AASTO Green Book—ecological functions were not included in the road's designated level of service. Street trees are referred to as FHO's, "fixed and hazardous objects", and the sidewalk is referred to as an "auto recovery zone", which doesn't

bode well for pedestrians. Streets traditionally outfitted with trees, like boulevards and avenues, fell out of favor and led to generations of street construction that lacks walkability and ecological functioning.

Excessive Cul-De-Sac Requirements
Minimize the required size of cul-de-sacs from the conventional 100-foot diameter. A diameter of 70 feet is ideal, depending upon the requirements of emergency vehicles. Allow the use of bioretention facilities at the center of cul-de-sacs or "hammerhead" turnarounds.

Lack of Requirements for Street Trees
Trees along streets soften the urban environment, reduce air pollution, cool ambient air temperatures, elevate property values, and provide shade and habitat. Many municipalities are adopting street tree requirements once again for new street construction. Local governments should incorporate cyclic pruning programs and tree planting standards in their street improvement specifications. Shade trees should be spaced at a distance equal to the mature crown width of the species selected (*Natural Resource Management in the Urban Forest*).

open space
Lack of Development Transfer Rights
Transfer of development rights is a commonly used financial tool to reward property owners for conservation of sensitive ecologies and critical open space. Property owners can sell the development potential of an undeveloped parcel to another property owner seeking more development capacity on their property. In exchange, the undeveloped property is held in conservation by the seller or deeded to a land trust for tax incentives to the property owner. However, state enabling legislation must be enacted to permit transfer of development rights.

Lack of Hillside and Tree Ordinances

Local hillside ordinances are an important conservation tool to protect property from systematic erosion and the resultant sediment loading of streams due to careless hillside development. Likewise, tree ordinances ensure stewardship of an area's forested and vegetated groundcover vital to management of watershed metabolism.

Lack of Waterbody Buffers

Vegetated buffers around significant waterbodies like wetlands, floodplains, lakes, streams, and rivers are important for maintaining vital ecological functioning and preventing untreated urban runoff from reaching waterbodies. Protective buffer widths and cross-section designs should be established in accordance with the waterbody's ecological significance.

Lack of Conservation Requirements

Many municipalities lack protection ordinances for environmentally critical areas on private property, particularly in wetland and aquifer recharge zones. Consider providing incentives and ordinances which encourage LID-sensitive development.

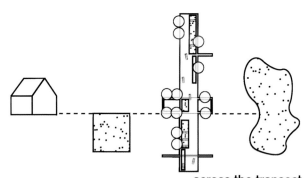

across the transect

LID as Non-Conforming Infrastructure

Permit the use of alternative stormwater management techniques by making LID a by-right development system. Incentivize LID, allowing developers to fast-track approval applications through the municipal planning process, as well as waive stormwater infrastructure impact fees.

Municipalities should seriously consider raising permitting fees for conventional developments while reducing permitting fees for LID developments since LID reduces stormwater management costs for municipalities.

Management, not Maintenance

Before, During, and After LID Construction

In LID, native vegetation and soils are designed to function as stormwater infrastructure. Clearly written LID management plans and protection measures are imperative for maintaining the long-term productivity of these systems. LID infrastructure may require creative land stewardship instruments related to conservation easements, dedicated parcels, land trusts, and property owner association covenants. Property owner education and involvement must be a part of all these strategies.

As with conventional ornamental landscapes, general management of LID facilities includes debris removal, weeding, erosion and sediment control, watering, pest management, and replacement of dead plant material during establishment periods of approximately three years. Most importantly removal of core vegetation and compaction of soils undermines functioning in LID infrastructure.

This manual does not specify vegetation because naturalized species and plant sociology vary widely among locales based on ecosystem characteristics. A local landscape professional, horticulturist, or nursery should be consulted prior to LID plant selection to determine applicable planting times, establishment protocols, spacing, and requirements for sun, shade, and soil.

Keep in mind that LID infrastructure models ecological behavior and is thus a constantly evolving landscape. LID landscapes "rewild" urban development, providing new levels of ecological services with highly varied floristic structures based on seasonal change. Since LID landscapes mimic naturally occurring ecosystems they will attract native wildlife as newly established systems diversify. Some opponents of rewilded landscapes perceive certain wildlife as pests (though most snakes will not chase you). However, wildlife attracted to LID landscapes prey on perceived pests as part of the nutrient cycling intrinsic to ecosystem balance. Wildlife rises to the level of a pest in the absence of ecosystem balance. Integrated pest management—based on ecosystem thinking—controls pests like mosquitoes with the introduction of bats and purple martins.

The following list notes other best practices supportive of LID stormwater management:

building

Protect Vegetation and Soil During Construction

Soil compaction is the leading cause of premature tree death in urban areas according to the World Forestry Center. Most tree root structures are located within three feet of the ground surface with the majority of root activity responsible for water and nutrient absorption occurring within 18 inches. Measures should be taken to protect existing and future planting areas from soil compaction during building construction. Delineate and monitor preservation areas on site as "no compaction zones" with proper fencing and signage.

Coordinate Among Construction Entities
Rather than clearcut and grade the entire site in conventional practice, several strategies can be undertaken through construction staging to minimize site disturbance. Clearing, grading, and heavy construction would ideally occur during the driest months and conclude before the wettest months, minimizing soil compaction, erosion, and sedimentation. Large projects requiring long periods of time would ideally be staged in segments to complete operations in one section to minimize erosion of exposed areas. Lastly, establish and maintain erosion and sediment controls during clearing and grading activities.

property

Develop a Site Protection Plan Using Efficient Site Design
Develop, implement, and enforce a site protection plan
beyond the minimum requirements legislated by state
water protection agencies. In lieu of grading the entire
site, grading can be reduced through the use of foundation
systems requiring minimal excavation. Minimize cut and fill
by orienting the long axis of buildings along contours. Limit
soil disturbance to only excavations for roads, utilities, and
building systems.

Amend Existing Soils
Conduct soil analysis to determine if soil has poor
organic or physical properties. Amend soil if necessary
using compost, biosolids, and other renewable organic
substances to improve porosity and infiltration rates. When
possible, favor existing permeable soils over imported soil
for LID facilities. Highly contaminated soils will require
additional bioremediation to eliminate toxicity.

Monitor and Manage LID Facilities
Inspection and management requirements for each LID
facility vary; therefore it is important to create a checklist
for each facility to determine the management schedule.
Since the primary infrastructural components are organic
facilities with widely varying lifecycles, facility checklists
should assess for performance criteria related to the
delivery of ecological services, sedimentation, water
quality, plant growth, health of indicator plant and animal
species, and overall ecological performance.

Designate Responsible Party for LID Management Plan
A responsible party, whether a property owner association
or a municipality in the case of public infrastructure, should
be designated to implement the LID management plan.
Implementation often entails periodic modifications of the
plan in response to the evolution of plant communities
and their pest cycles. The responsible party will need
to educate grounds crew and property owners on plan
implementation.

street

Coordinate Utility Infrastructure for Easy Access

Coordinate placement of both dry and wet utilities to use shared trenches and utility ducts, minimizing the environmental impact of installation and management. Shared trenches allow various companies to synchronize work and share expenses. Dry utilities, such as telephone, electric, and gas can be stacked vertically in the same trench, while wet utilities, such as potable water, greywater, and wastewater can share easements.

Use Trenchless Technology

Trenchless technology is an umbrella term covering a family of methods, materials, and equipment to maintain underground utilities without the need for excavation. Since trenchless technology involves non-invasive utility repair and upgrades it allows plant-based LID facilities to remain intact. This is important since LID facility performance improves over time as their attendant plant communities mature.

Provide Adequate Growing Space for Urban Street Trees

Root systems and their associated microbial communities are essential for the phytoremediation of polluted runoff and soil stabilization. In order to accomplish this, trees must be spaced properly for adequate root growth. Conflicts with streets, sidewalks, underground utilities, and overhead power lines should be minimized. Planting strips along streets should be six to eight feet wide. A good growing medium of sandy loam should be used in the planting area with underground perforated drains as required to remove excess water.

Use Structural Soils Where Appropriate

Structural soils are an engineered medium of aggregate and soil that creates a porous load-bearing system for drainage and root growth under pavements. Structural soil supports mature trees, and potentially increases their life expectancy at a rate of four to five times greater than the average urban tree.

Pervious Paving Management

Clogging from sedimentation is the main reason for pervious paving failure. Larger particles trap smaller particles in pore spaces, reducing a system's ability to provide infiltration. Sediment is deposited by vehicle and foot traffic, wind blown debris, and transported by stormwater runoff. Periodic management should include vacuum sweeping at least four times a year to clear pores in the top layer of pervious paving. Most municipalities already have vacuum sweeping equipment for their current street maintenance. Catastrophic clogging from flooding or inappropriate management can be remediated by spot-drilling half-inch holes every few feet through some paving systems. Estimated cost of management for these surfaces is equivalent to conventional paving systems, including inspections and vacuum sweeping treatments.

open space

Protect Native Vegetation

Mature native vegetation and healthy soil structure are necessary in normalizing watershed metabolism, including stable stream channels, wetlands, and healthy aquatic systems. Vegetative cover provides surface areas that dissipate peak stormwater discharge in urban areas. Natural resource planning should identify and protect critical areas based on ecological connectivity and biodiversity. Areas that should be protected include riparian corridors, floodplains, connected wildlife habitat areas, and common open space within developed sites.

Rehabilitate Impacted Areas

Disturbed areas may require soil enhancement and replanting with native trees and vegetation in order to achieve the full hydrologic benefits of the site. Consult with a qualified urban forester or landscape architect to develop a long-term vegetation and soil management plan.

Practice Controlled Burning

Controlled or prescribed burning is a technique used in forest management, farming, and prairie restoration. Fire is a natural component of nutrient cycling in some forest and grassland ecologies, and can protect trees from future disturbances related to fire, disease, and insects. The controlled burn prepares a seedbank for renewed growth, while improving habitat for wildlife species. Informing users and nearby residents of scheduled burns can help allay community concerns.

Where can you learn more?

Though this manual provides information regarding principles on implementing LID, it is by no means exhaustive. Consult the publications in the bibliography to find more extensive information regarding specific engineering criteria governing LID design. In addition to the literature cited, there are many websites with information complementary to the principles outlined in this manual.

glossary
pp. 214-221

bibliography
pp. 222-225

image sources
pp. 226-227

Glossary

100-year storm event
A flood event that statistically has a one percent probability of occurring in any single year. Based on expected stream flood stage levels during a 100-year storm event, an approximate area can be extrapolated that designates the 100-year floodplain.

aerobic
Living or occurring only in the presence of oxygen.

anaerobic
Living or occurring only in the absence of oxygen.

aquifer
An underground layer of permeable rock containing or conducting groundwater.

best management practice (BMP)
State-of-the-art measures to ensure effective and practical means of mitigating nonpoint source pollution.

bioretention facility
Depressions designed to mitigate pollutants from stormwater runoff by utilizing soil and vegetation. Examples of bioretention facilities include bioswales, rain gardens, and bioretention basins. Typically soils are amended with sand or compost depending on desired treatment function.

bioswale
An open, shallow, gently sloped, vegetated channel designed for stormwater treatment in which the primary pollutant mitigation mechanisms are filtration and phytoremediation by native grasses.

blackwater
Sewage containing bodily or biological wastes from toilets and industrial processes.

carrying capacity
In LID, the intrinsic capacity of a site's landscape to fully treat stormwater runoff loads.

constructed wetland
Constructed wetlands are artificial marshes or swamps with permanent standing water that offer a full range of ecosystem services to treat polluted stormwater.

detention
The temporary storage of stormwater runoff in ponds, depressed areas, or underground storage facilities that allow metered discharge to reduce peak flow rates.

detention pond
A stormwater catchment basin designed to temporarily hold stormwater runoff for metered discharge within a 24-hour period to a conveyance system or receiving waterbody.

dry swale or grass swale
An open vegetated channel used to filter and attenuate stormwater runoff, as well as convey stormwater downstream.

ecological services
Resources and processes that are supplied by natural ecosystems and serve all living organisms. The 17 ecological services of healthy watersheds are: atmospheric regulation, climate regulation, disturbance regulation, water regulation, water supply, erosion control and sediment retention, soil formation, nutrient cycling, waste treatment, pollination, species control, refugia, food production, raw material production, genetic resources, recreation, and cultural enrichment.

ecosystem
Clearly defined system of biogeochemical interactions among living organisms in a given area, including their nonliving (abiotic) interactions with their physical environments.

ecotone
A transitional zone between two adjacent but different plant communities where a high level of niche biogeochemical exchanges occur (e.g., interface of land and water).

emergent vegetation
Vegetation that is rooted below the mean water level but extends above the water level.

erosion control devices
Devices used to prevent and/or control excessive soil erosion of land surfaces. They can prevent excessive stream sedimentation and ecosystem damage.

evapotranspiration
The process by which water is transferred from the earth to the atmosphere through the combined processes of transpiration from plants and evaporation from waterbodies.

215

eutrophication

Reduction of dissolved oxygen in waterbodies due to concentrations of nutrients that stimulate excessive plant growth, such as algae and nuisance plants, eventually causing severe reductions in water quality and elimination of aquatic wildlife. Also known as "Dead Lake Syndrome".

facultative vegetation

Vegetation capable of functioning under varying hydrologic conditions, from wet to dry.

filter strip

A sloped medium that attenuates stormwater runoff by converting it into sheet flow, typically located adjacent and parallel to an impervious surface such as a roadway, parking lot, or driveway.

filtration

The separation of sediment from stormwater runoff through a porous media such as sand, a fibrous root system, or a man-made filter.

first flush

Initial stormwater runoff from impervious surfaces containing levels of concentrated pollution higher than that which occurs during the rest of the storm event.

floodplain

Areas adjacent to a stream or river that experience periodic flooding where floodwaters accumulate and dissipate their energy. The floodplain includes the floodway, which carries significant volumes of flood water, and the flood fringe, the area covered by flood. In the US, Flood Insurance Rate Maps (FIRM) map both the 100 and 500-year floodplains. Development is regulated within the mapped 100-year floodplain.

flow control devices

Devices used to regulate peak flow of stormwater, attenuating energy flow and volume.

greenway

A corridor of public open space used for recreation, pedestrian and bicycle traffic, often located along waterbodies.

greywater

Non-potable (non-drinkable) wastewater generated from dishwashing, laundry, bathing, and treated stormwater runoff that can be used to irrigate vegetation or flush toilets.

groundwater

Water that exists beneath the ground surface in soil pore spaces, factures of rock formations, underground streams, and aquifers; the source of water for wells and springs.

hard engineering
Conventional civil engineering systems reliant on mechanical, abiotic structures for infrastructural purposes. In LID, hard engineering refers to pipe-and-pond stormwater management for water storage and evacuation, which simply addresses throughput.

headwater
The source of a stream or river. Non-tidal rivers, streams, lakes and wetlands can become part of the surface tributary system that creates the headwater source, as long as the average annual flow is less than five cubic feet per second.

hydric soil
Relating to soils that are formed under conditions of saturation, flooding, or ponding long enough to develop anaerobic conditions in the subsurface layers.

hydrology
The study of the movement, distribution, and quality of water on the Earth and in the atmosphere, addressing both the hydrologic cycle and water resources.

impervious surface
A material unable to transmit fluids vertically through its surface.

industrial lawn
An area of turf grass, usually composed of a single non-native species mowed at a low, even height requiring energy-intensive maintenance, chemical fertilizers, and irrigation to maintain a uniform appearance.

infiltration
The vertical movement of stormwater runoff through soil, recharging groundwater stocks.

infiltration basin
A shallow impoundment with hydric soil that is designed to infiltrate stormwater, without retaining a permanent pool of water.

infiltration trench
A shallow excavation that is lined with filter fabric and filled with stone or aggregate to create underground reservoirs for stormwater infiltration.

integrated pest management (IPM)
Pest control that employs environmentally sensitive approaches, involving feedback from the local context to keep the number of pests low enough to prevent unacceptable damage and nuisance.

invasive species
Non-native species imported to an area, which negatively impact the local ecology by dominating competition for nutrients.

217

local species
Non-native, non-invasive species that have become naturalized to a specific ecosystem.

mesic soil
Soils characterized by, or adapted to, moderately moist soil conditions.

microbial
Of or relating to living microscopic organisms, such as bacteria, mites and fungi critical to nutrient cycling in ecosystems since they act as decomposers. These communities regulate biological functioning in soils and water.

native species
Species that are indigenous to a region or specific ecosystem.

nonpoint source (NPS) pollution
Surface level pollutants associated with human activities which can be collected and transported by stormwater runoff.

nutrient cycling
Biogeochemical process by which nutrients move through biotic and abiotic systems. For instance, nutrients are returned to the Earth after organic material decays or is eaten and excreted.

oversized pipes
A stormwater conveyance pipe that is sized larger than required to reduce peak flow rates.

peak load/flow rate
In stormwater management, the maximum water flow (water volume) or load (pollutant count) a stormwater system must manage during a storm event.

pervious paving
A material that is able to transmit fluids vertically through its surface.

pipe-and-pond system
Conventional stormwater management system that centralizes stormwater collection in a detention pond for discharge off site.

point source pollution
Pollution attributed to a single source, originating from an identifiable point, such as an industrial facility.

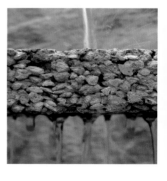

rain garden
A rain garden is a planted depression designed to infiltrate stormwater runoff, but not hold it.

rainwater harvesting
The recycling of stormwater runoff from roofs and other impervious surfaces.

refugia
An area that has remained unaltered by climatic, environmental and urban disturbances, making it a suitable habitat for remnant species.

retention
The storage of stormwater runoff on site to allow for sedimentation of suspended solids and minor treatment through biological processes.

retention pond
A constructed stormwater pond that retains a permanent pool of water and improves water quality through minor biological treatment.

riparian
Of or relating to the bank of a river or stream.

riparian buffer
A strip of hydric soils with facultative vegetation located along the banks of a river or stream offering niche ecotone services.

sediment
Particles of dust, soil, and debris; commonly referred to as suspended solids, deposited by water, wind, or ice.

sedimentation
A mechanical process in which suspended solids settle to the bottom of a waterbody under the influence of gravity.

shared streets
Multipurpose right-of-ways that create a common space to be shared by vehicles, pedestrians, and bicyclists, without conventional mode separators like lanes, sidewalks, and curbs.

smart growth planning
Planning model that advocates land uses supportive of compact, transit-oriented, walkable, and bicycle-friendly communities as a counter to suburban sprawl.

soft engineering
Ecological engineering systems that utilize biological processes and materials for infrastructural purposes. In LID, vegetation is used to filter, infiltrate, and treat stormwater, balancing both quantity of water throughput with quality.

storm event
Precipitation that occurs in different durations, amounts, and intensities, referred to in terms of a year (e.g. 100-year event).

stormwater management system
Infrastructure for runoff management from rain and snowmelt events through the use of flow control and detention facilities to prevent flooding.

stream scouring
The erosion of stream edges due to excessive water flows.

structural soil
An engineered medium of aggregate and soil that creates a porous load-bearing system for drainage and root growth under pavements, ensuring maximum plant health.

submergent vegetation
Vegetation that thrives completely submerged below standing water level.

surface sand filter
A sand filtering system consisting of surface and subsurface components for trapping nitrates, phosphates, hydrocarbons, metals, and sediment in the first flush of runoff.

treatment
In LID, processes that improve water quality by utilizing phytoremediation or microbial processes that metabolize contaminants in stormwater runoff.

tree box filter
A tree box filter or in ground well consists of a container filled with amended soil and planted with a tree, underlain by crushed gravel media.

turbidity
Cloudy or hazy appearance in water caused by the suspension of fine solids.

underground sand filter
Similar to a surface sand filter, except that the sand and underdrains are installed below grade in a concrete vault. Usually used where land availability limits the use of a sand surface filter.

underground detention
Below grade vaults for stormwater detention where land availability limits the use of surface stormwater management facilities.

upland vegetation
Plant communities in dry areas that are not directly associated with a body of water or hydric soils.

urban forest
Remnant tree stands in an urban setting in which the ecosystem is inherited from previously existing wilderness.

urban heat island effect
An atmospheric condition in which radiant heat and pollutants from urbanization create a confining layer that sequesters warm air, elevating temperatures by two to ten degrees Fahrenheit.

urban stream syndrome
Unhealthy stream flow regimes marked by chronic flash flooding, altered stream morphologies, elevated nutrient and contaminant levels, excessive sedimentation from eroded stream banks, and loss of species diversity.

vegetated wall or green wall
An architectural wall that is partially or completely covered with vegetation. Living walls integrate plant material and their growth media into the building envelope while green facades structurally host the growth of vines from the ground or planters.

vegetated roof or green roof
A roof veneer of living vegetation and soil matrix installed atop buildings. These systems offer indoor thermal regulation, stormwater storage, and heat island mitigation.

watershed
The geographical area drained by a river or stream. In the continental US there are 2,110 watersheds.

watershed approach
A resource management framework that addresses priority water resource goals, taking into consideration multiple stakeholder interests in groundwater and surface water management.

wet vault
An underground retention facility that provides storage of stormwater runoff where land availability limits the use of surface stormwater management facilities.

xeric soil
Soil characterized by, or adapted to, extremely dry soil conditions.

xeriscape
Water conserving landscapes planted with drought tolerant native species.

Bibliography

Books

Arendt, Randall G. *Conservation Design for Subdivisions: A Practical Guide to Creating Open Space Networks*. Washington, DC: Island Press, 1996.

Balmori, Diana and Gaboury Benoit. *Land and Natural Development (LAND) Code: Guidelines for Sustainable Land Development*. Hoboken, New Jersey: John Wiley & Sons, 2007.

Campbell, Craig S. and Michael H. Ogden. *Constructed Wetlands in the Sustainable Landscape*. New York: John Wiley & Sons, Inc., 1999.

Dramstad, Wenche E., James D. Olson, and Richard T. T. Forman. *Landscape Ecology Principles in Landscape Architecture and Land-use Planning*. Washington, DC: Island Press, 1996.

Farr, Douglas. *Sustainable Urbanism: Urban Design with Nature*. Hoboken, New Jersey: John Wiley & Sons, Inc., 2008.

Flores, H. C. *Food Not Lawns: How to Turn Your Yard into a Garden and Your Neighborhood into a Community*. White River Junction, Vermont: Chelsea Green Publishing Company, 2006.

France, Robert L. *Wetland Design: Principles and Practices for Landscape Architects and Land-use Planners*. New York: W.W. Norton & Company, Inc., 2003.

Girling, Cynthia and Ronald Kellett. *Skinny Streets & Green Neighborhoods: Design for Environment and Community*. Washington, DC: Island Press, 2005.

Izembart, Helene and Bertrand Le Boudec. *Waterscapes, Using Plant Systems to Treat Wastewater*. Land & Scape Series. Barcelona, Spain: Editorial Gustavo Gili, 2003.

Kibert, Charles J., ed. *Reshaping the Built Environment: Ecology, Ethics, and Economics*. Washington, DC: Island Press, 1999.

Kinkade-Levario, Heather. *Forgotten Rain: Rediscovering Rainwater Harvesting*. Springfield, MO: Granite Canyon Publications, 2004.

Low, Thomas E. *Light Imprint Handbook: Integrating Sustainability and Community Design*. Charlotte, NC: New Urban Press, 2008.

Metro. *Green Streets: Innovative Solutions for Stormwater and Stream Crossings*. Portland, OR: Metro, 2002.

Smith, Carl, Andy Clayden, and Nigel Dunnett. *Residential Landscape Sustainability: A Checklist Tool*. Oxford, UK: Blackwell Publishing, 2008.

Teyssot, Georges, ed. *The American Lawn*. New York: Princeton Architectural Press, 1999.

Websites and Manuals

Barr Engineering Company. *Minnesota Urban Small Sites BMP Manual*. St. Paul, MI: Metropolitan Council, 1993, http://www.metrocouncil.org/environment/water/BMP/manual.htm (accessed June 17, 2009).

Bentrup, Gary, USDA National Agroforestry Center. *Conservation Buffers: Design Guidelines for Buffers, Corridors, and Greenways*. Asheville, NC: Department of Agriculture, Forest Service, Southern Research Station, 2008, http://www.unl.edu/nac/bufferguidelines/docs/conservation_buffers.pdf (accessed March 17, 2009).

Brown, Hillary, Steven A. Caputo Jr., Kerry Carnahan, and Signe Nielson. *High Performance Infrastructure Guidelines*. New York: New York Department of Design and Construction, 2005.

Center for Watershed Protection, Inc. *Post-Construction Stormwater Model Ordinance*. Ellicott City, MD: 2008, www.cwp.org/Resource_Library/Model_Ordinances/index.htm (accessed September 18, 2009).

Chicago Department of Transportation. *The Chicago Green Alley Handbook*. Chicago: City of Chicago, 2006, http://brandavenue.typepad.com/brand_avenue/files/greenalleyhandbook.pdf (accessed April 1, 2010).

City of Portland. *Stormwater Management Manual*. Portland, OR: 2008 Revision, www.portlandonline.com/bes/index.cfm?c=47952 (accessed February 2, 2010).

Department of Environmental Resources, Programs and Planning Division. *Low Impact Development Design Strategies:*

An Integrated Design Approach. Largo, MD: Prince George's County, Maryland, 1999, http://www.epa.gov/nps/lidnatl.pdf (accessed January 2, 2007).

Elmendorf, William, Henry Gerhold, and Larry Kuhns. *Planting and After Care of Community Trees*. University Park, PA: The Pennsylvania State University, 2008, http://pubs.cas.psu.edu/freepubs/pdfs/uh143.pdf (accessed February 19, 2010).

Erwin, Patty S. and Sasha Kay. *Natural Resource Management in the Urban Forest*: Arkansas Forestry Commission: Urban Forestry Division, August 2000.

Hinman, Curtis. *Low Impact Development Manual for Puget Sound*. Tacoma, WA: Washington State University Pierce County Extension, 2005, http://www.psp.wa.gov/downloads/LID/LID_manual2005.pdf (accessed January 4, 2007).

Industrial Economics, Incorporated. *Green Parking Lot Case Study: Heifer International, Inc.*, 2007, http://www.epa.gov/region6/6sf/pdffiles/heiferparkingstudy.pdf (accessed March 19, 2010).

Low Impact Development Center, Inc. "Urban Design Tools: LID Design Examples." http://www.lid-stormwater.net/design_examples.htm (accessed March 8, 2010).

Mecklenburg County Water Quality Program. *Town of Huntersville Water Quality Manual*. Huntersville, NC: 2008, http://www.huntersville.org/Planning%20Info/Huntersville%20Design%20Manual%20January%201,%202008%20Version.pdf (accessed February 22, 2010).

Nataluk, Douglas M. and Richard Dooley. *The Practice of Low Impact Development*. Washington, DC: NAHB Research Center, Inc., 2003, http://www.lowimpactdevelopment.org/lid%20articles/practLowImpctDevel_jul03.pdf (accessed January 4, 2007).

Nisenson, Lisa. *Using Smart Growth Techniques as Stormwater Best Management Practices*. Washington, DC: United States Environmental Protection Agency, 2005, http://www.epa.gov/dced/pdf/sg_stormwater_BMP.pdf (accessed March 13, 2006).

Pushard, Doug. "Harvest H20.Com - the Online Rainwater Harvesting Community." www.harvesth2o.com (accessed March 18, 2010).

SEMCOG. *Low Impact Development Manual for Michigan: A Design Guide for Implementers and Reviewers*. Detroit, MI: Southeast Michigan Council of Governments, 2008, http://

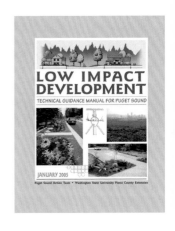

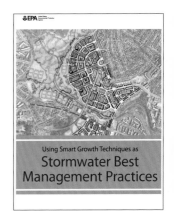

Using Smart Growth Techniques as
Stormwater Best
Management Practices

www.swmpc.org/downloads/lidmanual.pdf (accessed October 29, 2009).

Sharp, Randy, James Sable, Flavia Bertram, Eva Mohan, and Steven Peck. *Introduction to Green Walls Technology, Benefits and Design*. Toronto, Ontario: Green Roofs for Healthy Cities and Greenscreen, September 2008, http://www.greenscreen.com/Resources/download_it/IntroductionGreenWalls.pdf (accessed March 4, 2010).

Trinkaus, Steven D. *Town of Tolland Design Manual: Low Impact Development Stormwater Treatment Systems, Performance Requirements, Road Design, and Stormwater Management*. Southbury, CT: Trinkaus Engineering, LLC, 2008, http://www.tolland.org/wp-content/uploads/2008/02/lid-design-effective-2-1-2008.pdf (accessed March 19, 2010).

United Facilities Criteria (UFC). *Low Impact Development*. Washington, DC: United States Department of Defense, 2004, http://www.wbdg.org/ccb/DOD/UFC/ufc_3_210_10.pdf (accessed July 14, 2008).

225

Image Sources

All images are by UACDC unless otherwise listed. Every effort has been made to secure permission from owners for use in this manual. We apologize for any errors or omissions.

100 *Gingko*
Inoc - flickr.com

101 *Green Vase Zelkova*
Horticulture Society of New York

101 *Lacebark Elm*
Joseph O'Brien - USDA Forestry

101 *Red Oak*
Sledd Nursery

102, *Skinny Streets*
106-07 Kevin Robert Perry - City of Portland

102 *Green Streets*
Puget Sound Partnership

102, *Shared Streets*
112-13 Andy Fenstermacher

103, *Eco-Boulevards*
118-19 Steve Boland - sfcityscape.com

103 *Parkways*
IAMU - Lake County, IL

122-23 *Eastern Parkway*
Louisville Metro Parks

Open Space
140 *3B -Tanner Springs Park*
Mark Ace

140 *3C - Shaw Nature Reserve*
Melissa Keller

140 *3D - Fresh Kills Park*
New York Department of Parks and Recreation

141 *5A - High Point Garden*
Paul Symington

141 *4D - Wetland*
Svetlana Makarova

Facilities
149 *Permeable Weir*
Capitol Region Watershed District

149 *Curb*
Mike Houck - Urban Greenspaces Institute

149 *Tree Mound*
USEPA

159 *Slim Tank*
BlueScope Water

159 *Precast Septic Tank*
Community Restoration Foundation

159 *Bladder Tank*
Eco Sac

163, *Filter Strip*
216 Trinkaus Engineering

165 *Underground Sand Filter*
Ironsmith

169 *Vegetated Wall*
ELT Easy Green

173, *Porous Asphalt*
218 www.graniterock.com

173 *Grass Concrete Paving*
Bomanite Grasscrete Systems

173 *Turf Pavers*
Invisible Structures, Inc.

173 *Open Grid Pavers*
Adbri Masonry

175 *Infiltration Trench*
Lake County Stormwater Management Commission

177, *Tree Box Filter*
220 Filterra Bioretention Systems

179 *Rain Garden*
Carol Stream Engineering

183 *Bioswale*
Dr. Alan P. Davis

What Role You Play
198 *Turf Image*
Green Lawn Incorporated

204 *Emerald Necklace*
Google Maps

207 *Protect Waterbodies*
General Building Contractors of New York State

208 *Tree Protection*
W. Jacobi - Colorado State University Extension

209 *Trenchless Technologies*
Pipe Fusion Services

210 *Operations and Management*
worldsweeper.com

Glossary
215 *Grass Swale*
Thomas Engineering, P.A.

217 *Impervious Surface*
North Texas Grease Abatement Council

UNIVERSITY OF
ARKANSAS

Manual Team

**University of Arkansas
Community Design Center (UACDC)**
Stephen Luoni, Director
Steven L. Anderson Chair in Architecture and Urban Studies
Cory A. Amos, Project Designer
Katie Breshears, AIA, LEED AP, Project Designer
Jeffrey Huber, LEED AP, Project Designer
Cade Jacobs, Project Designer
Stephen M. Reyenga, Project Designer
Linda Komlos, Administrative Specialist
Deborah Guzman, Student Intern
Becky Roark, Student Intern

**University of Arkansas
Ecological Engineering Group**
Dr. Marty Matlock, PE
Sarah Lewis, Graduate Associate
Rusty Tate, Graduate Associate
Zara Clayton-Niederman, Research Associate

Fay Jones School of Architecture
Jeff Shannon, AIA, Dean

Manual Reviewers
Bobby Hernandez, USEPA Region Six
Dr. Carl Smith, CMLI, UA Department of Landscape Architecture
Christopher Suneson, ASLA, APA, LEED AP
Katie Teague, UA Agricultural Extension Services

Beaver
Water
District

Western
Branch

COMMUNITY FOUNDATION
OF THE OZARKS

with
OZARKS WATER WATCH™
UWRB:Upper White River Basin Foundation

National Center for
Appropriate Technology
www.ncat.org

Manual Sponsors

Funding was made available in part by the Arkansas Natural
Resources Commission (ANRC) through a grant from the United
States Environmental Protection Agency (USEPA) Region 6
Section 319(h).

Publication was made possible by generous support from:

Arkansas Forestry Commission's Urban Forestry Program
and US Forest Service

Beaver Water District
Lowell, Arkansas

Community Foundation of the Ozarks and
Stewardship Ozarks Initiative
Springfield, Missouri

Ozarks Water Watch with **Upper White River Basin Foundation**
Branson,Missouri

National Center for Appropriate Technology
Southeast Field Office: Fayetteville, Arkansas

US Green Building Council
Western Branch Arkansas Chapter: Northwest Arkansas

Illinois River Watershed Partnership
Northwest Arkansas and Northeast Oklahoma

"Our space planning should take its cue from the patterns of nature itself—the water table, the floodplains, the ridges, the woods, and above all, the streams."
William Whyte, *The Last Landscape*

©2010 **UACDC**, Fayetteville, Arkansas http://uacdc.uark.edu ISBN 978-0-9799706-1-0